INCLUSIVITY

⚘

A Gospel Mandate

More Orbis Books by Diarmuid O'Murchu

Adult Faith

Ancestral Grace

Consecrated Religious Life

Evolutionary Faith

God in the Midst of Change

In the Beginning Was the Spirit

The Meaning and Practice of Faith

Transformation of Desire

INCLUSIVITY

❧

A Gospel Mandate

Diarmuid O'Murchu, MSC

ORBIS BOOKS
www.orbisbooks.com

ORBIS BOOKS
www.orbisbooks.com

Fathers and Brothers
MARYKNOLL™

Founded in 1970, Orbis Books endeavors to publish works that enlighten the mind, nourish the spirit, and challenge the conscience. The publishing arm of the Maryknoll Fathers and Brothers, Orbis seeks to explore the global dimensions of the Christian faith and mission, to invite dialogue with diverse cultures and religious traditions, and to serve the cause of reconciliation and peace. The books published reflect the views of their authors and do not represent the official position of the Maryknoll Society. To learn more about Maryknoll and Orbis Books, please visit our website at http://www.maryknollsociety.org.

Library of Congress Cataloging-in-Publication Data

O'Murchu, Diarmuid.
    Inclusivity : a Gospel mandate / by Diarmuid O'Murchu.
        pages cm
    Includes bibliographical references.
    ISBN 978-1-62698-134-8
    1. Multiculturalism—Religious aspects—Christianity. 2. Church.
3. Church and minorities. 4. Ethnicity—Religious aspects—
Christianity. I. Title.
    BV639.M56O48 2015
    260.8—dc23
    2015002685

Contents

Introduction

*Jesus hung out with whores and social outcasts, was
remarkably casual about sex, disapproved of the family,
urged us to be laid back about property and possessions,
warned his followers that they too would die violently,
and insisted that the truth kills and divides as well as
liberates. He also cursed self-righteous prigs and deeply
alarmed the ruling class.*

—TERRY EAGLETON

Every Christmas, Christians recreate the crib with a vulnerable baby lying in a shabby inn, possibly a shepherd's cave. On Christmas Day itself, Christian worship all over the world echoes to the words "He came to his own and his own received him not" (John 1:11). From the beginning he was destined to be the archetypal outsider.

But was he? Was his welcome into the world tinged with rejection from the very beginning? Was he always an outsider, whose rejected status would become the basis for its very opposite? Or was there a much more subtle message right from the start? Did Jesus himself benefit from a radical inclusive welcome, thus paving the way for a thrust that characterizes the Judeo-Christian message from the very beginning? This is the stance adopted by the popular writer Nick Page (2011, 23ff.), which I will use to launch us into the inclusive vision explored in the present book.

In the cultural context of the time, Joseph's family home would have been the first option for Mary to give birth. It may have been a crowded household with a little space in the "kataluma" (meaning: inn or guest room). So they laid the baby elsewhere in the house, perhaps in a manger or animal feeding trough. The homes at the time often consisted of a two-floor division, humans sleeping upstairs and animals occupying the ground floor during the night.

According to Nick Page (2011, 24), "The story of Jesus's birth, therefore, is not one of exclusion, but inclusion. . . . Joseph's relatives made a place for Jesus in the heart of their household. They did not shun Mary, even though her status would have been suspect and even shameful (carrying an illegitimate child): they brought her inside. They made room for Jesus in the heart of a peasant's home."

Among the first guests who came through the door were shepherds. Here the Gospel inclusivity is categorically declared. Shepherds were social and religious outcasts, ritually suspect and socially disreputable. According to the Mishna, it was forbidden for orthodox Jews to buy wool, milk, or kids directly from herdsmen. Many of them were homeless and deprived of basic human rights. Yet, here they are as the first to welcome the one who in time would declare himself to be the Good Shepherd.

From the beginning Jesus was the beneficiary of Torah-inspired hospitality and inclusivity. These were to be the outstanding features of his entire life, and the long-neglected basis of his public life and ministry. The one who was welcomed into the world with the warmth and hospitality of his Jewish home would devote his public life to the establishment of that same inclusivity, but this time with horizons that few formal religions, including his own Jewish culture, could embrace. His public life and ministry had inclusivity inscribed at its very core.

Christianity stands or falls on its fidelity to the outsider. Jesus himself clearly transgressed many of the Messianic expectations of the time. He did not fit the divine triumphalism or the kingly expectations. He was born out of wedlock, with what seems to have been an unpretentious childhood; and as a rebellious young adult, he chose not to marry, something that marked him as a traitor to his culture and an aberration to his religion.

His parabolic language threw many into confusion, and his transgression of Jewish propriety caused no small measure of consternation. Eventually the system could no longer tolerate his empowering message and got rid of him in a quick brutal death. But that did not end his maverick status. The outsider rebounded, convincing the women (the first disciples) that he was more radically alive in death than during his earthly existence.

Despite its early attempts to gain recognition and status as a formal religion embedded in Greek culture, Christianity once more opted for the outsider. The Gentiles, and not the "chosen" Jewish people, became the foundation stone of the future church. Institutionalization was inevitable as happens in every major organization; not until the fourth century, however, did Christianity lose sight of the outsider when Constantine laid the foundations for Christianity's adoption as the official religion of the Roman Empire—the greatest betrayal Christians have ever known.

But the outsider lost no time in launching a counter-culture. The early monastics fled to the desert places, declaring unambiguously their allegiance to the outsider status. Many such groups would honor the prophetic vision through the subsequent decades of Christian history.

This is a book for outsiders, for the millions around the Christian world, attracted to the vision and praxis of Jesus, but disenchanted with the power games of Christendom, and a church excessively wedded to power, pomp, and prestige. The book also addresses those who feel they don't fit in, either because of alternative vision, more earth-grounded concerns, or minority status resulting from race, ethnicity, social standing, or sexual orientation.

The book has a special concern for those in our time who seek an integration of faith around their adult capacities, seeking fellowship and interaction that honor the adult in a mutual and inspiring way, as people seek discipleship with an adult Jesus in the service of an adult God. The outsider in today's church is not only the one who thinks or behaves differently, but increasingly it is those who seek to outgrow the childish dependency of old in favor of a new engaging mutuality that prioritizes and calls forth the adult in the contemporary world.

Chapter 1

All the Talk about Chosen People

He drew a circle that shut me out,
Heretic, rebel, a thing to flout.
But love and I had the wit to win;
We drew a circle and took him in.

— Edwin Markham

Jesus pronounces throughout his ministry: those who are
sure they are in are shown to be out, and those who are
sure they are right are shown to be wrong. All who were
hoping that the Messiah would come and sanction the
traditional religious and cultural norms of their society
must have been gravely disappointed.

— Kristin Johnston Largen

In my international travels over the years, I am intrigued by people's special interest in my Irish origins, particularly by people
whose ancient ancestors came from "the island of Saints and
Scholars." Ireland is my home country, and I wish at times I could

feel as enamored and attached as many of those who admire it from a distance. While Ireland is, and always will remain, my homeland, my interaction with other peoples and cultures has significantly changed how I view my national identity. From a foundational formation in Irish republicanism and sectarian Catholicism, I have evolved into a global citizen with an identity that I no longer wish to reduce to any one nation, culture, or religion.

Deep in my psyche, the echoes still endure of "the island of Saints and Scholars," a kind of chosen people, unique and unparalleled among the peoples of the earth. And our oppression under colonial occupation reinforced that sense of insular superiority. In the late twentieth century, it morphed into another violent uprising between the Catholics (republicans) and the Protestants (pro-British) in Northern Ireland. Had I not joined a Religious Order (in 1970), there is a distinct possibility I would have joined the Irish Republican Army in its attempt to oust the British from my homeland.

For me, the drastic conversion happened in 1975. I was traveling by train in the United Kingdom, sitting beside two young men who initiated a conversation by (1) informing me that they were British soldiers and (2) that they were on their way for military duty in Northern Ireland. Resentment boiled up within me, but since all other seats on the train were occupied, I had no choice but to stay where I was seated and participate in the ensuing conversation. Gradually, I warmed to their sincerity, friendship, and hospitality (they offered me some of their sandwiches and chocolates). We parted with a warm hug. I wished them well and genuinely hoped that someday we might meet up again.

But that meeting would never happen. Three days later on the front page of all British newspapers were their photos—killed in action in Northern Ireland, brutally murdered by my fellow countrymen. It was the first time in my life that I experienced deep grief. I bled within, and found it difficult to contain my rage and disgust. My attachment to the island of Saints and Scholars was changed forever. I was launched into becoming a global citizen, with the earth itself as my sacred nation and all humankind as my chosen people.

With such a background I tend to react negatively to religious claims for superior status. My earliest faith development asserted that I belonged to the chosen people of God, a claim I gradually came to associate with my Judeo-Christian origins. Of course, in time, I came to realize that every major religion makes such claims, reinforced more dogmatically in the monotheistic religions of Judaism, Christianity, and Islam. According to the popularized Jewish version, those occupying the land of Israel are God's *Chosen People*. God has selected these people as the exclusive beneficiaries of God's special favor, and through God's involvement with this specific people, salvation (redemption) can be realized for all peoples of every tribe, nation, and religion.

Jewish Presuppositions

Historically, both Jews and Christians have used the claim to great effect not only to exalt Judaism and Christianity above all other religions, but also to exclude and undermine those deemed to be outside the realm of divine favoritism. As a conviction—and for many an indisputable truth—it creates the foundation and justification for the ideological superiority that both Judaism and Christianity have often claimed. Paradoxically, it has also contributed to the anti-Semitism that has tarnished Christianity throughout the two thousand years of Christendom. It is questionable if anybody has gained from this claim to a unique and exalted status.

Most Jews hold that being the Chosen People means that they have descended from the family of Abraham, Isaac, and Jacob, and have been given a special role on earth to fulfill God's design for humanity. Israel is the name God gave to Jacob, the son of Isaac, and grandson of Abraham. "Thou shalt not be called any more Jacob, but Israel shall be thy name. And he called him Israel. And said to him: I am God Almighty, increase thou and be multiplied. Nations and peoples of nations shall be from thee, and kings shall come out of thy loins" (Gen. 35:10–11).

In the Old Testament, Israel stands for the religious covenant community, the people who worship God in spirit and in truth. Secondarily, it denotes a distinct ethnic group or nation that is chosen to become the spiritual Israel. Decisive for the Old Testament prophets and their prophecies is the theological quality of the "people of God," not their ethnic and political characteristics.

Traditional proof for Jewish "chosenness" is found in the Torah, the Jewish Bible, particularly in the book of Deuteronomy in which Israel is described as God's "treasured people out of all the people on the face of the earth" (Deut. 7:6). In Deuteronomy 14:2, we read, "For you are a holy people to Hashem your God, and God has chosen you to be his treasured people from all the nations that are on the face of the earth." Throughout the Book of Deuteronomy there are many allusions to this special divine choice. And from Genesis 17: 7, "And I [God] will establish my covenant between me and you [the Jewish people] and your descendants after you in their generations, for an everlasting covenant, to be God to you and your descendants after you." Jewish scholar, David Novak (1995, 163) captivates this exclusive emphasis when he writes,

> Any attempt to see this relationship (the covenant) as some sort of contract, some sort of bilateral pact between autonomous parties, is clearly at odds with biblical teaching. In the Bible, God alone is autonomous, and God alone can make initiatory choices without impunity. Israel's only choice seems to be to confirm what God has already done to her and for her. . . . For Israel, there are no multiple options, as we understand the term today.

For the Jews, therefore, there is a generational aspect to "chosenness." They see themselves as the natural descendants of Abraham, via Isaac, and subsequently via Jacob (whom God renamed *Israel*). There is a further nuance to this chosenness: God expected His chosen people to strictly follow His moral laws and not follow the evil ways of their neighbors. This they would do through their allegiance to the covenant, translated in Hebrew as *Berit*, occurring 286 times in the Hebrew Bible. Depending on the context, it can be translated as "treaty," "pact," "agreement," "solemn promise," "obligation," or more familiarly as "covenant." It is referred to thirty-three times in the New Testament.

With the rise of Christianity, the doctrine of Israel as the Chosen People acquired an added polemical edge against the background of the claim of the Church to be the "true Israel" and the guardians of God's chosen people. While some Jewish scholars such as Rabbi Mordecai Kaplan, founder of the small but influential Reconstructionist movement, wanted to get rid of the notion of chosenness, it has become more deeply ingrained, particularly for orthodox Jews. In times of persecution it served as reinforcement for solidarity and resistance. On other occasions, including the recent conflict with Palestine, it became the basis of a superior nationalistic ideology endowed with a lot of violence, oppression, and the destruction of life and property.[1]

Inflated Monotheism

To many contemporary peoples, the notion of God favoring one nation or people above all others sounds ideological, preposterous, and reminiscent of religion's worst forms of oppression. And it is difficult to press the rhetoric into an inclusive claim, as sought by Frank Spina (2006, 6) in the following quote:

God did not choose Israel in order to preserve Israelites while condemning all others. That is not the way either election or exclusion works in the Old Testament. Israel was not chosen in order to keep everyone else out of God's fold; Israel was chosen to make it possible for everyone else eventually to be included. It would be a mistake to construe Israel's exclusive election as a function of its superiority. On the contrary, Israel's exclusive status is completely a function of what might be called God's exclusive status.

What God are we describing here? And where have we obtained this understanding from? *Monotheism* enters our reflections.

In religious scholarship (especially in the West) the evolution of monotheism is widely considered to be a development of maturity leading to deeper truth. Monotheism promotes the idea that God should be regarded as a unified wholeness. This can translate into an understanding of God as solely one—person or entity—as in the Muslim faith, or as a combination of descending expressions all accountable to one source (also called henotheism). In the case of Christianity, despite its belief in three "persons" named Father, Son, and Holy Spirit, there has always been a clear understanding that the diversity of the three is unambiguously subservient to the one overriding reality that Christians call *God*.

The rise of monotheistic religion is usually attributed to the Egyptian pharaoh, Akhenaton, in the fourteenth century BCE. Although the evidence is circumstantial, it seems that Moses, who lived around that time, assimilated this concept of one God, taking it into the desert with him. Thus the Jewish religion—and its key notion of the Chosen People—developed along monotheistic lines, as did Christianity and Islam in later times. However, Assmann (2010, 31) claims that the juxtaposition of monotheism and polytheism is a much later development, arising from the theological debates of the seventeenth and eighteenth centuries. For some, the opposite of monotheism is not polytheism (worshipping many Gods), but the worship of false idols, thus failing to honor the one true God, the origin of unifying truth. The worship of false idols leads to false truths, while—according to monotheistic religion—allegiance to the One God provides a more reliable pathway to unifying truth.

Jon Assmann (2010) suggests that the real opposite of monotheism is not polytheism but *cosmotheism*, the religion of an immanent God, which polytheistic belief systems strive to uphold by proposing various expressions of the divine in the divergent aspects of the created world. For Assmann therefore,

> The divine cannot be divorced from the world. Monotheism, however, sets out to do just that. The divine is emancipated from its symbiotic attachment to the cosmos, society, and fate, and turns to face the world as a sovereign power. In the same stroke humanity is likewise emancipated form its symbiotic relationship with the world, and develops in partnership with the one God. (Assmann 2010, 41)

Thus the monotheistic deity reinforces the long history of patriarchal domination in a belief system that claims there can only be one unambiguous source for divine and earthly power. Effectively this translates into a system that disempowers and disenfranchises not only humans, but the living earth itself and the divine presence immanent in the whole creation. To this extent, monotheism resembles a political ideology rather than a religious belief, one that reinforces exclusion and undermines all attempts at genuine inclusivity.

The Chosen Outsider

As we shall see in subsequent chapters of this book, Jesus consistently chooses and prioritizes the outsider: the fishermen, the sick, the poor, the disenfranchised, the Samaritans. St. Paul presses the inclusivity even further by embracing all those labeled as *Gentiles*. We end up with what is inescapably a counter-cultural vision to that of the Chosen People: The Christian dispensation does not tolerate any outsiders, but much more seriously, it is the outsiders who become the catalysts for a radical new quality of inclusivity. Such inclusivity is not compatible with any form of exclusivity, religious or otherwise.

To reclaim this foundational truth of the Christian faith, there is a great deal of religious and cultural clutter that needs to be cleared away. Clearing the ground needs to begin with the notion itself of the Chosen People. Underpinned by a desire to prioritize humans as God's special—and superior—creatures, the concept rests on a number of foundational claims that do not stand up to contemporary scrutiny, cultural or religious. In the desire to embrace elements like a special nation, an exclusive people, and a monotheistic God, we have construed a religious system that is now seen not only as outdated and dangerous, but unable to inspire and empower a more authentic sense of faith for the twenty-first century. The following are some of its more obvious short-comings:

1. A Reductionistic Cosmology. Despite the panoramic view of creation, described in the opening chapter of the book of Genesis, the grandeur and meaning of creation are largely suppressed. Obviously, the evolutionary and cosmological information at our disposal today was not available to those who compiled the Genesis narrative, and in the light of that more advanced understanding, we must challenge forthrightly their tendency (desire) to use the creation story as a lead up to humanity's superiority. By adopting such a reductionistic view of creation—in cosmic and

planetary terms—the author(s) of Genesis effectively excludes all
else for the sake of giving exalted status to the human. Creation
eventually ensues as an object for humans to use for their own
will and benefit. The modern notion of humans belonging intimately to creation—and having no authentic value without the
surrounding web of life—is a divine cosmic imperative that is
seriously undermined by the notion of Jewish chosenness.

2. *Patriarchal Religiosity.* Much of the material in the opening chapters of Genesis can be understood as a reflection on the
aftermath of the Agricultural Revolution, which commenced
around 8000 BCE. The previous foraging lifestyle gradually gave
way to a more structured mode of farming, with the streamlining
of land and property into segments managed by specific owners
(cf. Barker 2009). This led to various conflicts, the resolution for
which required even more stratification. The land became ever
more objectified, a resource to be conquered and used for material benefit, and the stratification led to a new elite managerial
culture dominated by controlling males. Some suggest that previous agricultural development was much more organic and egalitarian with females in leading roles (e.g., Eisler 1987), a claim
that is difficult to verify objectively to the satisfaction of modern
scholarship. The ensuing male dominance emulated—some say
created—the patriarchal God who ruled from above the sky, and
thus patriarchal religion became the established form of religious
belief. It was this quality of patriarchal religion that gave birth to
the notion of the Chosen People.

3. *Divine Imperialism.* The Sky God of the patriarchal era
was understood to be one of kinglike status, with an unquestioned divine right to rule and control. Therefore, the ideal representative on earth of this God was the ruling male king. The
great patriarchs of the Old Testament belong to this genre. The
covenant adopted in the name of the Chosen People required
absolute obedience and submission to the godly king, and when
the people failed to live up to such allegiance, they needed a

new divine rescuer, first embodied archetypally in the great king David, from which Christianity has conventionally claimed that Jesus was descended. And for much of the Christian era, the divine right of kings dictated the ethos and culture of the Christian faith. In this context, the notion of the Chosen People carries several imperial and oppressive elements, tending to favor divinely approved winners, and generally denouncing losers as religious infidels.

4. *A Distorted Anthropology.* In this analysis, anthropology has been distorted almost beyond recognition. The only true human is the imperial conquering male, expected to be God's obedient servant and faithful alloy, but in such a power-riddled dispensation, it is impossible to avoid intergroup, and interpersonal conflict. So, prevalent is the conflict that the Old Testament ideology projects the problem back into heaven, attributing the source of the problem to a battle between warring angels in heaven itself. This kind of anthropology inevitably becomes so destructively incestuous that a divine-rescue plot has to be concocted, and the messianic ideology takes over from there. Meanwhile, we lost sight completely of God's long empowering and inclusive befriending of human becoming (evolution) transpiring over several millennia, as illustrated by modern paleontology and science (more in O'Murchu 2012). The notion of the Chosen People is postulated not only on a corrupted anthropology, but also on one that blasphemously undermines both divine and human creativity.

5. *A Violent Spirituality.* Our human collusion with violence, in the name of a governing patriarchal God, is described at length in the works of the French scholar, Rene Girard. Throughout the Old Testament we encounter a God frequently engaged in battle with adversarial forces. In most cases, God is on the side of the victor and rarely in solidarity with the loser, as is typically the case in the New Testament. Whatever its initial inspiration, the notion of the Chosen People has fomented the patriarchal

desire to conquer and dominate, and to validate incarceration and bloodshed in a way that makes it increasingly difficult for contemporary Christians to believe in the notion of a God of peace and reconciliation. And that violent undercurrent has also seeped into the Muslim faith, where it has been liberally used in a new and increasingly violent interpretation of jihadist spirituality.

From Exclusive Nation to Inclusive Community

Despite Christendom's long allegiance to the ideology of a Chosen People, the time has come to sever the historical links and return to a more primordial wisdom that never adopted this ideology in the first place. As I shall indicate in a later chapter of this book, it is the haunting shadow of Constantine's addiction to patriarchal power that lies at the root of Christian exclusivity. From the fourth century onward, Christianity colluded with imperial religiosity and progressively became enmeshed in warfare, violence, oppression, sectarianism, and exclusion. Correspondingly, it lost sight of its original inspiration, its radical prophetic inclusivity, and its counter-cultural paradigm of inclusive, empowering community.

In the language and vision of the Gospels, this community is described as the *Kingdom of God*, which against the Aramaic background translates better as the *Companionship of Empowerment*. It is based on a worldview that is all-embracing in cosmic and planetary terms; it forthrightly condemns and revises all posturing at patriarchal domination; it turns imperial kingship on its head, replacing it with an empowering kinship; it invokes a radical incarnational anthropology inclusive of peoples of every race, creed, and color; and it counters all semblance of violence in favor of nonviolent liberation.

For Jesus, the primordial disciple of this new empowerment, there are no chosen nations, tribes, or peoples. All are equally embraced, and all have a place at the open table of universal life. For far too long, we Christians have compromised this foundational vision, largely because we have espoused a God who has been made the object of our patriarchal projections of election and exclusion. That is not the God of Christian faith but a divine caricature sanctioned by a patriarchal religiosity that has long outlived its usefulness. Its replacement is the long-neglected vision of the New Reign of God, the inclusive horizons of which are described in the subsequent chapters of this book.

Chapter 2

Love Your Enemies

It cannot be stressed too much: love of enemies has, for our time, become the litmus test of authentic Christian faith.

— WALTER WINK

The old law of an eye for an eye leaves everyone blind. It is immoral because it seeks to humiliate the opponent rather than win his understanding.

— MARTIN LUTHER KING JR.

The call to love even our enemies is Christianity's perennial challenge to the outsider. We must embrace with renewed fervor the very one (person or group) we would dearly love to destroy or eliminate. Those we wish to consign to the farthest away places, we must reach out to in a spirit of forgiveness, reconciliation, and unmitigated love. The grudges that may have smoldered deep in our hearts for months or years, we must submit to the possibility of healing and reconciliation. There is no room for excluded outsiders in the discipleship of Jesus.

Nietzsche rejected the command entirely, arguing that love of one's enemies is weakness and dishonesty. Mao Tse-Tung also wrote a commentary on this precept, arguing that universal love is an ultimate goal but that it is impossible until the class system is removed.

The key text underpinning the reflections of this chapter is that of Matthew:

> You have heard that it was said, "Love your neighbor and hate your enemy." But I tell you: Love your enemies and pray for those who persecute you, that you may be sons of your Father in heaven. He causes his sun to rise on the evil and the good, and sends rain on the righteous and the unrighteous. If you love those who love you, what reward will you get? Are not even the tax collectors doing that? And if you greet only your brothers, what are you doing more than others? Do not even pagans do that? Be perfect, therefore, as your heavenly Father is perfect. (Matt. 5:43–48)

Matthew seems to be reflecting an earlier strand echoed in 1 Thessalonians 5:15 and Romans 12:14, 17–20: Do not pay back evil. John Piper (1979, 34–35) notes that the negative command to renounce retaliation is never found in the New Testament without the corresponding positive command to behave proactively. What is not clear is the Old Testament influence on Matthew. The opening line of the above passage: "You have heard that it was said, 'Love your neighbor and hate your enemy' " does not actually occur in the Hebrew Scriptures. Rather it must have been a colloquial saying that had accrued added significance within a culture eager to oust the invading Roman forces.

It is also noteworthy that the Greek word used to translate love is that of *agape*, not the word, *stergein* (denoting love for a family member) or *eros,* the word often employed to denote sexual love, nor *philia* (denoting intimate human love). *Agape* denotes a quality of unconditional love, which we usually attribute to the Godhead itself. Conceptually, it seems to be the nearest we can get to describing divine love, an insight also adopted by Piper (1996, 174) who observes that enemy-love requires "a renewed mind which can prove the perfect will of God. Jesus called for a transformation so radical that it left nothing in a man untouched." Peace activist, Jim Forest (2014) describes it as an active love requiring our devoted and unceasing attention.

Indeed, the love required to reach out to the hated other is only possible "by the grace of God." It is a love that requires an altruistic disposition that comes easily to nobody. It is one of those challenges in the face of which we rightly say, "Were it not for the grace of God, it could not be achieved." We must add without hesitation, St. Paul's reassuring words: "My grace is sufficient for you." (2 Cor. 12:9). And such reassurance reinforces the challenge and requires us to accept it with even greater commitment.

The Lex Talionis

Scholars, ancient and modern, consider the love for one's enemies to be the supreme challenge of Christian faith. Without this radical embrace, the great commandment to love God and one's neighbor loses its originality and empowering depth. Some scholars argue that love of one's enemy is what separates Christianity from all earlier religions. The exact wording does not appear in prior Jewish texts, but there are examples of previous thinkers sharing Jesus' sentiments. Catholic scholar John P. Meier (2009, 531, 550, 573) quite categorically claims that the saying has no precedent in previous thought, secular or religious:

> The laconic and disturbing command, "Love your enemies," finds no exact iteration in the Old Testament or Qumran, or inter-testamental literature prior to A.D. 70,

or even in literature that is especially relevant to this topic, namely, pagan philosophical works. By "exact iteration" I mean that no parallel, however, close in thought or spirit, uses the terse, stark juxtaposition of the ever-popular direct imperative "love" with the impossible object "enemies." . . . Nowhere though in the huge amount of material that ancient parallels provide us do we find the terse, direct disturbing command, "Love your enemies." . . . The troubling content is embodied in a troubling formulation, all the more forceful for its brevity and originality . . . [This command] goes back to the historical Jesus.[1]

The *lex talionis* (an eye for an eye) predates the Hebrew Scriptures, running through the Babylonian law code of Hammurabi (c. 2285 BC) but much more developed than in earlier sources. The *lex talionis* is stated explicitly three times in the Old Testament. First, in Exodus 21:22–25, it is cited in a way that protected a pregnant woman and her child from death or injury that might occur if two men were in a fight. Second, in Leviticus 24:17–22, it is applied generally to any case where a crime of murder or intentional maiming occurred, indicating that the law applied by judicial authorities to both capital punishment and maiming punishments to be carried out in kind. Third, in Deuteronomy 19:15–21, it occurs in a passage to prevent perjury and using the court to execute or punish an otherwise innocent individual.

The introduction of the *lex talionis* into the Mosaic law for the nation of Israel and the ruling authorities is generally considered to be an advancement for the cause of justice designed to prevent personal actions of retaliation and revenge. The injured person or relative of the injured person could go to the governing judicial authority in Israel and seek justice. But what should the appropriate punishment be in the case of murder or maiming?

This is where the law comes into play: "a life for a life," "an eye for an eye," "a tooth for a tooth." The punishment must fit the crime—no more than the crime but also no less. It was strict but fair. It was also designed to prevent and deter such crimes. It was there to remove punitive actions for crimes from the hands of the victim and his family and put them into the hands of the governing judicial system. It was designed as a principle of proportional justice that would also guarantee appropriate punishment for the offender.

Commentators also claim that the *lex talionis* was, for ancient societies, an imposition of mercy. In its attempt to be just, and to be seen to be just, it signified the limitation of vengeance without diminishing the value of the human person. In prescribing a visible, realizable, and equitable response to injustice, the *lex talionis* sought to prevent disproportionate responses along with a pattern of unending retribution.

The Larger Context

Both John Piper (1979) and Lisa Sowle Cahill (1994) suggest that the unique Christian flavor of love your enemies is not to be found in transcending the many acts of violence described in the Hebrew Scriptures, but rather in the primordial vision of the Kingdom of God, as Christianity's foundational guide to living righteously. Cahill (1994, 27) goes on to suggest that the Sermon on the Mount provides the discerning context for a more responsible interpretation of what the command may have meant originally and its significance for Christian belief in our time.

The Sermon on the Mount—with its many lofty ideals—may be understood in any or all of the following contexts:

- A perfectionist code in line with the legalism of Rabbinic Judaism.
- An impossible ideal meant to drive the believer first to desperation and then to trust in God's mercy.

- An interim ethic, for the last days described by St. Paul and also endorsed by Jesus (according to some scholars).
- A deeper conversion enabling the believer to embrace more authentically life in the New Reign of God (the Kingdom). This latter view was originally propounded by Joachim Jeremias (1958) and subsequently adopted by several contemporary scholars.

The challenge and call to love one's enemies therefore is a new requirement exceeding the balancing-out envisaged in the *lex telionis* but also inaugurating a more courageous and pro-active commitment to the righteousness—peace and justice— already highlighted in the Jewish Torah. What is new therefore in the injunction to love enemies does not abrogate what we inherit from the Hebrew Scriptures but invites deeper levels of integration in how the injunction is to be lived out in daily life. And central to this novel integration is a quality of radical inclusiveness, much more explicit and demanding than we find in the requirements of Torah (the Jewish law).

When Jesus therefore declares, "Think not that I have come to abolish the law and prophets; I have come not to abolish them, but to fulfill them" (Matt. 5:17), these words tend to be heard as Jesus clinging on to every detail of the older dispensation while translating it afresh for a new moment. To which we must ask, "What makes the moment *new*, and what precisely is its *novelty*?" Perhaps the answer to that question can be located in the statement that rounds off that same paragraph in the Gospel of Matthew: "For I tell you, unless your righteousness exceeds that of the scribes and Pharisees, you will never enter the Kingdom of Heaven" (Matt. 5:20).

What is the new righteousness about? Are we looking at novel ways of implementing the great commandment to love God and neighbor, as already commanded in the Hebrew Scriptures, and indeed in every major religion known to humanity?

Or are we confronted with a challenge and invitation toward strategies that require more overt empowerment, more extensive inclusiveness, more mutual embracing of differences? Is there something extra at stake—what Paul Riceour (1976) calls *a surplus of meaning*—precisely because Christians are called to commit unflinchingly to establishing on earth the New Reign of God (the Kingdom)?

We can press these questions further as we seek to discern the meaning of unconditional love. All religions view this as the supreme quality of God, and the ultimate aspiration of all human desire and longing. Yet, every religion has ended up laying down conditions. No religion has taken seriously the invitation to unconditional love. Is this not the very quality that makes Jesus unique, the very quality that posed such a disturbing threat to the dominant forces of his day, Roman and Jewish alike? The radical inclusiveness arising from such unconditional love is what underpins the provocative practice of the open table, the infringement of purity laws, the blatant disregard for imperial power, the reconceptualization of family links, and above all, the command to love even one's enemies. There is a surplus of meaning here outstretching not only the Jewish faith, but indeed all the other major religions that exist today.

Ambivalent Christian History

Jesus did not turn out to be the Davidic warrior-king expected by many Jews—nor must his solidarity with the oppressed people of his day be reduced to that of a mere social activist. Jesus responded to evil with *nonviolent resistance*. Unlike the Zealots and others seeking to oust the Romans by violent methods, Jesus embraced a more radical critique, creating among his apostles, disciples, and followers an inclusive liberation and empowerment, inviting Jews, Gentiles, Samaritans, men, women, rich, poor, slave, and free into a new sense of freedom and release from bondage and slavery.

From earliest times, it seems that Christians opted for non-violent resistance, refusing to cooperate with the violent ideology of the empire. Not a few ended up enduring martyrdom because of their pacifist stance, an act of defiance that both intrigued and baffled the Roman imperial forces of the time (see the fine analysis of Moss 2013, 163ff.). Tertullian and Origen are often cited as the more noted pacificists of early Christianity, a radical nonviolent option that began to wane with the approval of the just war theory by St. Augustine and others in the fifth century.

The quintessential explanation of just war theory in the ancient world is found in Cicero's *De Officiis* (bk. 1, secs. 1.11.33–1.13.41). The Christian outline is usually traced to St. Augustine of Hippo (d. 430). Augustine did actually support the ideal of Christian pacifism, while interpreting love your enemy as demanding a change of *attitude* rather than external action. Thomas Aquinas saw it as a *counsel* rather than a precept for right action, an interpretation also adopted by Martin Luther and John Calvin. Thus we detect a series of accommodations resulting in an enviable watering down and domestication of the original Gospel ideal.

Christianity never entirely lost its nonviolent foundational aspiration, which in itself indicates a primordial, archetypal truth whose enduring authenticity will always challenge Christians (and others) to embrace the difficult ideal of loving one's enemies. Many movements have arisen seeking to reclaim this foundational Christian aspiration, and paradoxically it was in reference to this ideal that Mahatma Gandhi uttered his oft-quoted critique of Christian faith: "I like your Christ, I do not like your Christians. Your Christians are so unlike your Christ."

Nonviolent resistance is a method of social change that employs strategies such as strikes, sit-ins, boycotts, and civil disobedience, uniquely exemplified in the occupy movement of the early twenty-first century (see the valuable reflection of Thistlethwaite 2013). The nonviolent theory was developed by Henry

David Thoreau in his essay, *Civil Disobedience* (1849). Thoreau's argument that it was morally justified to peacefully resist unjust laws inspired Americans involved in the struggle against slavery and the fight for trade union rights and women's suffrage.

Many humans today are acutely aware of the violence in our world, and they feel a sense of helplessness and frustration on how to confront and change it. In truth, most humans live peaceably and pursue convivial engagement on a daily basis within a rapidly changing multicultural world. Critics, such as the late Christopher Hitchens, Richard Dawkins, and Sam Harris, point out that religion is a major cause of violence in our world, and despite the robust defense the religions try to make, I largely concur with that perception. In both subtle and overt ways, religion colludes with—and is frequently invoked to justify—our violent engagement with humans and with the living planet itself.

As a Christian people, we need to confront our ambivalence around violence and our centuries-long collusion with violent imperial structures and political strategies that have us now wedded to historical baggage that will not easily be discarded. We have not taken seriously the nonviolent mandate inscribed at the heart of our faith and unambiguously asserted in the command to love the enemy both within and without. Our credibility as people of faith in the twenty-first century largely depends on our attempts to translate anew into word and action the unconditional inclusivity of our Christian faith forever seeking reconciliation, peace, and unity with friend and foe alike.

Nonviolent Resistance

Apart from the key statement already examined—love your enemies—there are several passages in the Gospels inspiring and evoking a commitment to nonviolence.[2] To the fore is the description of the New Reign of God, with its "violent" inbreaking, as recorded in Luke 16:16: "The law and the prophets were until John; since then the good news of the kingdom of

God is preached, and every one enters it violently." Matthew 11:12 offers a related but different rendition: "From the time of John the Baptist until now the kingdom of heaven has suffered violence and people of violence take it by force." For Scripture scholars, this has long been regarded as a difficult text. William Barclay (Matthew's Commentary) suggests that we get close to the intended meaning by combining both versions of the saying: "Always my kingdom will suffer violence; always savage people will try to break it up, and snatch it away and destroy it. Therefore, only the one who is desperately in earnest, only the one in whom *the violence of devotion matches and defeats the violence of persecution* will in the end enter into it" (emphasis mine).

This interpretation should not be regarded merely as a metaphorical gloss. It strongly resonates with the language and nuance of parable narrative. It also carries poetic echoes pointing us to alternative understandings evoking imagination and intuition. It implies a call to conversion—a change of heart—at both personal and social levels. The personal implications echo strongly in this passage from a public lecture in 2007 by the theologian, James Alison (www.jamesalison.co.uk/texts/eng50.html).

"Love your enemies and pray for those who persecute you" means

> do not be towards them as they are towards you, for then you will be run by them, and you and they will become ever more functions of each other, grinding each other down towards destruction. Don't pay them the tribute of giving them that sort of free rental space in your soul. Instead of that, allow your identity to be given to you by your Father who is in heaven, who is not in any sort of reciprocity with them, and is able to be towards them as one holding them in being and loving them, without reacting against them. Given that you can't do this by a simple act of decision, you will require that your whole pattern of desire, formed in reciprocity

be turned around, and the only way to do that is to pray for them. For in praying for them you are beginning to allow the pattern of desire which is God to enter into your life, so allowing you to recognize your similarity with your enemies, rather than your exaggerated differences. This enables you to relativize the way you are towards your enemy, and will eventually empower you to be towards your enemy as God is. Thus you will be free of any contagion from their violence towards you.

It is the subtle nature of this contagion that needs further analysis and redress; as illustrated compellingly by peace activist, Jim Forest (2014). The research and reflections of the late Walter Wink are particularly insightful and contribute significantly towards integrating the inner non-violent disposition of the heart with the outward reach for peace and reconciliation. Wink directs us to the Sermon on the Mount as the primary basis for nonviolent, inclusive love. He begins by reminding us that the life and ministry of Jesus embraced an unambiguous commitment to nonviolent praxis:

> The God whom Jesus reveals refrains from all forms of reprisal and demands no victims. God does not endorse holy wars or just wars or religions of violence. The reign of God means the complete and definitive elimination of every form of violence between individuals and nations. (Wink 1992, 149)

Yet, Jesus was not passive in the face of injustice and evil. To the contrary, Jesus reveals a way to fight evil with all our power without becoming violent ourselves. *It is a way—the only way possible—of not becoming what we hate.* Jesus abhors both passivity and violence. He articulates, out of the history of his own people's struggles, a way by which evil can be opposed without being mirrored, the oppressor resisted without being emulated, and the enemy neutralized without being destroyed (Wink 1992, 189).

Three memorable injunctions occur in Matthew's Sermon on the Mount, which, for Walter Wink, captivate the nonviolent vision of Jesus: "Do not resist one who is evil. But if anyone strikes you on the right cheek, turn to him the other also; and if anyone would sue you and take your coat, let him have your cloak as well; and if anyone forces you to go one mile, go with him two miles" (Matt. 5:39–41). The statements are loaded with irony and parody, and the richly nuanced meaning can easily escape the average hearer.

On each of the three challenges, I rely extensively on the insights of Walter Wink (1992) since I know of no other commentary that illustrates so lucidly and vividly the counter-cultural nonviolent dynamic.

1. *If anyone strikes you on the right cheek* . . . "Why the *right* cheek? A blow by the right fist in that right-handed world would land on the *left* cheek of the opponent. An open-handed slap would also strike the left cheek. To hit the right cheek with a fist would require using the left hand . . . The only way one could naturally strike the right cheek with the right hand would be with the back of the hand. We are dealing here with insult, not a fistfight. The intention is clearly not to injure but to humiliate, to put someone in his or her place. . . . A backhand slap was the usual way of admonishing inferiors. Masters backhanded slaves; husbands, wives; parents, children; men, women; Romans, Jews. We have here a set of unequal relations, in each of which retaliation would invite retribution. The only normal response would be cowering submission. Why then does he counsel those already humiliated people to turn the other cheek? *Because this action robs the oppressor of the power to humiliate.* The person who turns the other cheek is saying, in effect, "Try again. Your first blow failed to achieve its intended effect. I deny you the power to humiliate me. I am a human being just like you. Your status does not alter that fact. You cannot demean me" (Wink 1992, 175–76).

Such a response would create enormous difficulties for the striker. Logistically, how would he hit the other cheek now turned to him? He cannot backhand it with his right hand (one only need try this to see the problem). If he hits with a fist, he makes the other his equal, acknowledging him as a peer. But the point of the back of the hand is to reinforce institutionalized inequality. Even if the dominant one orders that the other person should be flogged for such cheeky behavior, the point has been irrevocably made. Notice has been given that this subordinate is, in fact, a human being. In that world of honor and shaming, the dominator has been rendered impotent to instill shame on a subordinate. He has been stripped of his power to dehumanize the other. As Gandhi taught, *The first principle of nonviolent action is that of noncooperation with everything humiliating.*

2. *If anyone would sue you for your outer garment . . .* Matthew and Luke disagree whether it is the outer garment (Luke) or the undergarment (Matthew) that is being seized. But the Jewish practice of giving the outer garment as a pledge (it alone would be useful as a blanket for sleeping) makes it clear that Luke's order is correct, even though he does not preserve the legal setting.

Indebtedness was endemic in first-century Palestine. Jesus' parables are full of debtors struggling to salvage their lives. Heavy debt was not, however, a natural calamity that had overtaken the incompetent. It was the direct consequence of Roman imperial policy. It is to this situation that Jesus speaks. His hearers are the poor and disenfranchised. They share a rankling hatred for a system that subjects them to humiliation by stripping them of their lands, their goods, finally even their outer garments.

Why then does Jesus counsel them to give over their undergarments as well? This would mean stripping off all their clothing and marching out of court stark naked! Nakedness was taboo in Judaism, and shame fell less on the naked party than on the person viewing or causing the nakedness (Gen. 9:20–27). In his now naked state, the debtor has brought the creditor under the same prohibition that led to the curse of Canaan. Imagine him leaving the court, naked: his friends and neighbors, disgusted and angry, join his growing procession, which now resembles a victory parade. Imagine the guffaws that would ensue. There stands the creditor, covered with shame, the poor debtor's outer garment in the one hand, his undergarment in the other. The tables have suddenly been turned on the creditor. The debtor had no hope of winning the case; the law was entirely in the creditor's favor. But the poor man has transcended the plight of humiliation. He has risen above shame. At the same time he has registered a stunning protest against the system that created his debt in the first place.

Jesus provides here a hint of how to take on the entire system by unmasking its essential cruelty and burlesquing its pretensions to justice. Here is a poor man who will no longer be treated as a sponge to be squeezed dry by the rich. He accepts the laws as they stand, pushes them to absurdity, and reveals them for what they have become. He strips naked, walks out before his fellows, and leaves this creditor, and the whole economic edifice that he represents, stark naked.

3. *Go the second mile.* Jesus' third example is drawn from the relatively enlightened practice of limiting the amount of forced or impressed labor that Roman soldiers could levy on subject peoples to a single mile. Such forced service was a constant feature in Palestine from Persian to late Roman times. This forced labor was a source of bitter resentment by all Roman subjects. It is in this context of Roman military occupation that Jesus speaks. He does not counsel revolt. One does not "befriend" the soldier, draw him aside, and drive a knife into his back. Jesus was surely aware of the futility of armed insurrection against Roman imperial might; he certainly did nothing to encourage those whose hatred of Rome was near to flaming into violence.

But why carry his pack a second mile? Is this not to rebound to the opposite extreme of aiding and abetting the enemy? Not at all! The question here, as in the two previous instances, is how the oppressed can recover the initiative and assert their human dignity in a situation that cannot for the time being be changed. The rules are Caesar's, but how one responds to the rules is God's, and Caesar has no power over that.

Imagine then the soldier's surprise when, at the next mile marker, he reluctantly reaches to assume his pack, and the civilian says, "Oh no, let me carry it another mile." Why would he want to do that? What is he up to? Normally, soldiers have to coerce people to carry their packs, but this Jew does so cheerfully, and will not stop! From a situation of servile docility, the oppressed have once more seized the initiative. They have taken back the power of choice. The soldier is thrown off balance by being deprived of the predictability of his victim's response. He has never dealt with such a problem before. Now he has been forced into making a decision for which nothing in his previous experience has prepared him. If he has enjoyed feeling superior to the vanquished, he will not enjoy it today. Imagine the situation of a Roman infantryman pleading with a Jew to give back his pack!

The humor of this scene may have escaped us, but it could scarcely have been lost on Jesus' hearers, who must have been regaled at the prospect of thus discomfiting their oppressors. Jesus does not encourage Jews to walk a second mile in order to build up merit in heaven, or to exercise a supererogatory piety, or to kill the soldier with kindness. He is helping an oppressed people find a way to protest and neutralize an onerous practice despised throughout the empire. He is not giving a nonpolitical message of spiritual world transcendence. He is formulating a worldly spirituality in which the people at the bottom of society or under the thumb of imperial power learn to recover their humanity.

To those whose lifelong pattern has been to cringe before their masters, Jesus offers a way to liberate themselves from servile actions and a servile mentality. And he asserts that they can do this before there is a revolution. There is no need to wait until Rome has been defeated, or peasants are landed and slaves freed. They can begin to behave with dignity and recovered sense of humanity now, even under the unchanged conditions of the old order. Jesus' sense of divine immediacy has social implications. The reign of God is already breaking into the world, and it comes, not as an imposition from on high, but as the leaven slowly causing the dough to rise (Matt. 13:33; Luke 13:20–21). Jesus' teaching on nonviolence is thus of a piece with his proclamation of the dawning of the reign of God.

In the conditions of first-century Palestine, a political revolution against the Romans could only be catastrophic, as the events of 66–73 CE would prove. Jesus does not propose armed revolution. But he does lay the foundations for a social revolution, as Richard A. Horsley (2003) and others have pointed out. And a social revolution becomes political when it reaches a critical threshold of acceptance; this, in fact, did happen to the Roman Empire as the Christian church overcame it from below.

The Islamic Love of Enemy

It is sometimes claimed that love your enemy is not only in Christianity, but also in Islam. Not really. The Koran adopts the principle of an "eye for an eye" claiming to have inherited it from the Jewish Scriptures. The principle of *lex talionis* is explicitly stated in the Koran (5:45), "In the Torah, we prescribed for them a life for a life, an eye for an eye, a nose for a nose, an ear for an ear, a tooth for a tooth, an equal wound for a wound: if anyone forgoes this out of charity, it will serve as atonement for his bad deeds. Those who do not judge according to what God has revealed are doing grave wrong." Shi'ite countries adopting Islamic *Sharia* law tend to take literally the rule of an eye for an eye. Islam prides itself on being more about justice and fair play. Love is good, but it is more important that justice be done. If someone hits you, you have the right to hit them back. Islam leaves it up to you to decide. That's the general gist of it.

In terms of loving one's enemies, Islam distinguishes three categories of enemy. First are those regarded as personal enemies, maybe at work or even within the family itself; in this context, turning the other cheek is appropriate and even recommended as forgiveness is a highly cherished virtue. Second are territorial enemies like an unfriendly neighboring country or an potential invading force (type B). These you deal with like any nation deals with an enemy threat, following the rules of war, self-defense, etc. In this regard pacifism is not an authentic option. And there is a third type of enemy (type C), those perceived to be the enemies of the religion of Islam. Someone who insults Islam in public or tries to prevent the spread of Islam (by pen or by force) is to be silenced by submission or eliminated by force, with no limits envisaged for the violence that may be used.

Confronting Our Violent Collusions

Every believing Christian, Jew, and Muslim—as well as adherents of other major religions—endorses the universal command to love and consequently denounces acts of violence against all others, including those who may disagree with them. Yet, nobody can deny that every religion carries baggage of a violent nature, and many religions are highly ambivalent on how they engage the challenges to peace, forgiveness, and reconciliation. The following are among the urgent issues awaiting redress, if we stand any hope of (1) confronting our subverted violence and (2) eliminating its contagion from our beliefs and practices.

1. All the religions need to make public apologies for historical violence used to denounce or eliminate so-called heretics, many of whom are now seen to have been conscientious objectors whose goal was the purification of corrupt or bankrupt religiosity, or, in several cases, victims of distorted or perverse religiosity. The violence against women is a cultural scar still festering from age-old

religious oppression, as indeed is the violent exclusion targeting oppressed minorities such as Jews, mystics, homosexuals, etc.

2. All religions need to humbly acknowledge the ongoing subtle collusions with violence, far more common than most of us care to acknowledge. Most Christian churches give covert endorsement to the just war theory. Currently, the Muslim faith is probably the most overt in its jihadist ideology, with its various cultural incarnations in different parts of Africa and the Middle East. Both Muslims and non-Muslims are likely to object to my identifying one particular religion and will be quick to point out that the Koran does not tolerate violence of any type.

   Every religion makes blanket claims of this nature. In its original purity each religion embraces and endorses several noble aspirations. All religions, however, have been culturally influenced and, in most cases, have embraced culturally infiltrated values to degrees that no religion seems honest or transparent enough to admit. Scholars on the one hand, and religionists on the other, adopt and promote an original purity of belief naively implying that it is actually an enduring reality, when in fact it is not. It never is! The enduring practice is always influenced and frequently heavily contaminated by cultural influence. There can be no breakthrough to a more authentic religion—in this case to less violent articulations—without first taking seriously and wrestling with such collusive cultural influence.

3. The ideology of kingship still haunts many of the major religions. In Christianity this translates into liturgical language of a highly idolatrous and oppressive nature, totally alien to the Gospel vision of the Kingdom of God (the subject material of Chapter 4). Such imperial

language is particularly blatant in Christian hymnology, where God and Jesus are frequently lauded in exaggerated imperial language, often casting the divine power as the victor who destroys and eliminates the enemy.[3]

4. Prayer formulas, sanctioned over time, also need to be reassessed for the collusion with violence, in both word and aspiration. To the fore are the Psalms themselves with the many allusions to conquering and eliminating enemies, and a military-type God who favors those who win in battle and whose enemies are frequently portrayed as being on the losing side, and therefore deserving of the violent punishments attributed to them by God. This divine punitive figurehead features strongly throughout the Hebrew Scripture, despite the protests of Old Testament scholars that the real God of the Hebrews was the peace-loving deity of the covenant and not the military-type figurehead who populates many pages of the Hebrew Scriptures.

5. The violent ideology that underpins Christian history is often traced back to the Roman Emperor Constantine (272–337) but tends to ignore the salient violence innate to the Greek culture that so strongly influenced the Gospels themselves along with Christian lore of the early centuries. Greek metaphysics and epistemology, with its heavy emphasis on rationality, logic, and binary dualisms, created a kind of indoctrination that led to several adversarial conflicts. Despite his critique of Aristotle, St. Thomas Aquinas continued to describe God with some distinctive patriarchal attributions: omnipotent, omniscience, impassible, immaterial, immutable. This language reinforced the notion of a God over-against, all-powerful as distinct from powerless (sinful) humans. It was a matter of time until such a powerful deity was declared to be head of the army, the one who reinforced

every violent victor, religious and political alike. Christianity stands little hope of being a world force for peace and reconciliation without a radical abandonment of such violent collusion.

The challenge to love the enemy without is likely to cut little ice in Christianity until the churches themselves face the momentous task of confronting the enemy within. Whatever the original cause, few can deny that the contemporary church is deeply infiltrated with violent collusion. It shows up in overt language and in covert expressions of power and domination. Coming to terms with the inimical forces within would seem to be a nonnegotiable for any credible attempt at reclaiming the radical inclusivity embodied in the Gospel command to love everybody unconditionally and particularly those we seek to exclude and oppress as enemies.

Chapter 3

Compassion Shatters Boundaries

Compassionate love is counter-cultural. It creates upheavals in the ways we understand ourselves, others, and the world. Compassion does not just alleviate suffering, but rather transforms it. Compassion helps us to experience what justice feels like.

— Maureen O'Connell

Compassion is a word often used to describe the heartbreak of seeing another suffer unjustly. It is sometimes described as having pity for the others, sharing their pain and anguish, but like the suffering-others feeling unable to do anything to change their plight. It carries strong emotional weight, translating into concern, pity, and solidarity.

Etymologically, compassion signifies standing in solidarity with the other's suffering, feeling within oneself something of the other's pain and trauma. It denotes deep empathy, whether felt at a distance or conveyed in a more tangible way. Derived from the original Latin, the English noun compassion, meaning *to suffer together with*, is based on the noun *patior* (to suffer) from which arises words like patient, and *pathos*, indicating intense suffering. In short, compassion may be described as the understanding or empathy for the suffering of others with a desire to help them find release from the suffering.

In what I consider to be a comprehensive and inspiring study, Maureen O'Connell (2009, 3, 51) describes the call to a more compassionate way of living in these words: "Compassion is not comfortable and private but rather dangerous and political. . . . Compassion unleashes the interruptive and liberating power of contrast experiences and hones our ability to feel, to imagine, and to enact alternatives to what is."

Religious Significance

For Karen Armstrong (2011), compassion is the outstanding unifying force among the great world religions. It is the active wing of the universal desire to love unconditionally (often described as the Golden Rule). Despite various nuances of meaning in different religious systems, all religions embrace and promote love as the great unifying force, the core spiritual value shared by all the religions we know today.

In 2009, Karen Armstrong, supported by sympathetic colleagues around the world, launched the *Charter for Compassion* (www.chaterforcompassion.org), inviting people of all creeds and none to work together, adopting the fundamental principles of universal justice and respect, with the Golden Rule as an ethical core. In its final paragraph the charter states as follows:

> We urgently need to make compassion a clear, luminous and dynamic force in our polarized world. Rooted in a principled determination to transcend selfishness, compassion can break down political, dogmatic, ideological and religious boundaries. Born of our deep interdependence, compassion is essential to human relationships

and to a fulfilled humanity. It is the path to enlightenment, and indispensable to the creation of a just economy and a peaceful global community.

Far beyond the conventional use of the word, compassion here denotes a social force for harmony and solidarity, a political value fostering economic and structural justice, a nonviolent power for reconciliation, healing, and more enduring peace, and a spiritual concept that seeks to transcend the divisive polarizations of sectarianism and religious ideology. This all definitively reinforces the inclusiveness being explored in the present work.

Compassion features strongly in all the great world religions (see the comprehensive overview of Balslev and Evers 2010). In *Hinduism* we note an evolutionary historical development from yogic traditions of introspection to theistic traditions of devotion, maturing in time into the great medieval compendiums of dharma, the sacred world order. In this latter context, compassion denotes a quality of spiritual integrity that seeks the good of others through nonharming (nonviolence), service, charity, and social obligation. The personal and systemic harmonize around the reconciling and unifying power described as compassion.

A vast literature exists on the Buddhist notion of compassion, which translates as two words, *karuna* and *metta*, the former being the better known. *Metta* denotes a disposition of loving kindness and a benevolence toward all beings free of selfish attachment, while *karuna* means mercy, active sympathy, gentle affection and a willingness to bear the pain of others. In the *Wisdom of Compassion*, the Dalai Lama describes *karuna* as a strong disposition of nonjudgment toward, and acceptance of, all others, particularly those deemed to be outcasts or marginalized.

According to the Buddha, compassion crushes and destroys the pain of others. Compassionate action shelters and embraces the distressed. While it carries a primary meaning of sentiment and feeling, it is of a quality and depth that cannot but translate into practical action. And such action is inclusive of all, particularly those excluded by oppression and marginalization.

In Judaism, compassion is one of the central attributes of the divine, and one of the core obligations of humanity. Several commentators note that in Hebrew, compassion translates as *râcham* (verb) and as *racham* (noun), which also means *womb*, thus describing God's love for the people in terms of maternal care and affection. The Hebrew Bible describes God as both compassionate and merciful: "The Lord! The Lord! A God compassionate and gracious, slow to anger, abounding in kindness and faithfulness" (Exod. 34:6). God forgives Israel's iniquity and restrains His wrath as a result of His mercy (Ps. 78:38). The Israelites are commanded to "walk in God's ways" (Deut. 8:6), and the rabbis interpret this to suggest that compassion is the highest form of Godlike behavior. For the Italian Jewish scholar Samuel David Luzzatto (1800–65), compassion was the "first foundation" of Judaism, an innate quality, constituting the basis of love, kindness, and righteousness, and the benevolent actions that ensue, particularly toward all who suffer in any way.

Islam adopts a root word similar to the Hebrew *racham*, the Arabic *rahman* and *rahim*. Each of the 114 chapters of the Koran, with one exception, begins with the verse, "In the name of Allah the Compassionate, the Merciful." A good Muslim is to commence each day, each prayer and each significant action by invoking Allah the Merciful and Compassionate, that is, by reciting *Bism-i-llah a-Rahman-i-Rahim*. The Muslim Scriptures urge compassion toward captives as well as to widows, orphans, and the poor. *Zakat*, a toll tax to help the poor and needy, is obligatory upon all Muslims deemed wealthy enough to do so (calculated by assessing the net wealth of an adult at the end of a year (Koran 9:60). One of the practical purposes of fasting during the month of Ramadan is to help one empathize with the hunger pangs of those less fortunate, to enhance sensitivity to the suffering of others and develop compassion for the poor and destitute.

Gospel Compassion

As a unifying force, adopted by all the great religions, compassion denotes a disposition of nonjudgmental acceptance and loving care. It is primarily a sentiment of the heart that seeks to embrace and empower those adversely affected by life's circumstances and particularly those victimized by unjust pain and suffering. If the authentic desire for compassion was truly released into the world, then we probably would rid our world of warfare, oppression, and exploitation. This has not happened because often the sentiment does not translate into action; and when it does, it is frequently restricted to one's own religious group. Compassion is a liberating and empowering potential that every religion has subverted to one degree or another.

And perhaps most culpable of all is Christianity! In its Gospel usage, compassion denotes a great deal more than emotion or sentiment. It is a bold subversive claim to justice and empowerment beyond the crippling legacy that suffering often entails. In the Greek New Testament, it translates as *splangnezomai*. The word occurs seventeen times in the New Testament, applied to Jesus on eight occasions. In Greek, it literally means *being moved from the depths of one's bowels*. It is a strong visceral word and when applied to Jesus in the Gospels, the Greek reads as a verb, not as a noun. In other words, compassion is not only a caring feeling or disposition. More accurately, it is an inner enlightened quality of response that requires action to rectify the wrong being felt or perceived. Compassion is about what one feels compelled to do and not only the horror one feels.

In Gospel terms, compassion should never be rendered as *mercy* or *pity*. Statements like showing mercy to another, or having pity upon somebody, evoke a patronizing concern very different from the Greek, *splangnezomai*. Gospel compassion seeks out *empowerment*, a resolution to human suffering requiring an examination of what caused the suffering in the first place, how it can now be rectified, and how a more liberating resolution can be guaranteed for the future. This goes far beyond the immediacy of personal plight, trauma, and suffering. It seeks to address cultural and systemic factors. It considers how social, economic, and political forces facilitate or inhibit empowering deliverance. In a word, it is strongly related to the pursuit of justice.

Many years ago, Scripture scholar, Marcus Borg, made the bold suggestion that Jesus deliberately chose compassion as an antidote to the ritual purity code of the inherited Jewish tradition.[1] He suggests that the Lukan text "Be compassionate as your Father-God is compassionate" (Luke 6:36) provides a counter-cultural shift from the Levitical guideline: "Be holy as God is holy." Borg rightly describes this as a paradigm shift in our understanding of Christian discipleship:

> The central quality of the community of Jesus can also be seen in the paradigm or core value which was meant to shape its life. The dominant paradigm structuring his social world was, "Be holy as God is holy "(Lev. 19:20) with holiness understood as purity. Jesus echoed this passage even as he deliberately contrasted it by substituting compassion: "Be compassionate as God is compassionate (Luke 6:36). . . . Concern with purity intrinsically creates boundaries; the life of compassion intrinsically reaches across boundaries. Like the Spirit, of which compassion is the primary fruit, compassion shatters boundaries. In short the Jesus movement was a community of compassion, and to take Jesus seriously means to become part of such a community. (Borg 1994a, 154)

How to translate the compassionate endeavor into liberating action is further explored by Marcus Borg in his book *Meeting Jesus Again for the First Time* (1994b) wherein Chapter 3 is entitled "Jesus, Compassion, and Politics." Here Borg claims that the compassion so evident in the teaching and in the public life of Jesus was more than a quality of God and an individual virtue: it was a social paradigm, the core value for life in community. In the Judaism of Jesus' time, holiness required various degrees of separation from everything unclean ensuing in a society structured around a purity system. All too quickly this led to the few deemed worthy to be included and the many deemed to be unworthy and therefore always condemned to be outsiders. This distinction and division has no place within a dispensation of Gospel compassion.

Solidarity for Inclusion

Gospel compassion is also the antidote to the cultural phenomenon of honor versus shame, apparently a dominant feature in the culture of the time. Social scientist, Bruce J. Malina is an oft-cited authority on this aspect of early Judeo-Christian culture (see Malina 2001) There are two kinds of honor—ascribed honor and achieved honor. Ascribed honor is the value given to a person in public based on one's family, bloodline, and heritage. On the other hand, achieved honor is the value or worth given to a person based on what one has accomplished—usually through some form of competition or challenge; rivalry or warfare can also be part of this (cf. Neyrey 1998, 15–16). Both forms demand and enhance a divisive culture of insiders versus outsiders.

The "in-groups" consist of one's household, one's extended family, and one's friends and neighbors; everyone else belongs to the "out-groups." In-group members were expected to be loyal to one another and ensure that all their members honored the cultural/religious expectations. Certain social and financial benefits accrued to the advantage of the in-group, reinforced by strong demands to keep outsiders well beyond the socially and religiously defined pale.[2]

Jesus challenges the honor-shame social code by a linguistic devise known as a *riposte*, defined by Neyrey (1998, 20) as "a quick clever reply to an insult or criticism." There are four steps to this protocol or social code of challenge and riposte, what might be described as a "push-and-shove" strategy: (1) claim of worth or value, (2) challenge to that claim or refusal to acknowledge the claim, (3) riposte or defense of the claim, and (4) public verdict of success awarded to either claimant or challenge. On the one hand, Jesus subversively claims honor, in terms of his new empowering and inclusive mission, while at times fiercely challenging all the social codifications that hindered or blocked his prophetic, liberating vision.

Gospel-based compassion tolerates no outsiders. It embraces and seeks to bring in all who are marginalized, oppressed, and excluded from empowering fellowship. It evokes a double response requiring a reawakened heart that knows it cannot withhold the just action that liberates and empowers. The transformation of the heart, which might also be described as the contemplative gaze, asks us to go where it hurts, to enter into places of pain, to share in brokenness, fear, confusion, and anguish. Compassion challenges us to cry out with those in misery, to mourn with those who are lonely, to weep with those in tears. Compassion requires us to be weak with the weak, vulnerable with the vulnerable, and powerless with the powerless. Compassion means full immersion in the condition of being human.

As a key dimension of Gospel inclusiveness, compassion must never stop short at what I describe in Chapter 9 as *the devotion of consolation*. The suffering plight of the other becomes an emotional entrapment, with a subtle lure into a kind of codependent befriending in which I use the pain and trauma of the other to comfort or console the unresolved inner pain of my own life. This is liberating neither for myself nor the other, and the ensuing inclusivity is actually a form of collusive oppression. Gospel compassion, on the other hand, desires the empowerment and liberation of the other with a freedom whereby the other can choose options for self-empowerment, thus forging interconnections that can catalyze breakthrough for others as well.

Nor must Gospel compassion be too closely identified with the traditional Christian notions of salvation and redemption, fueling another kind of codependency that breeds guilt and unworthiness. As Tom Drake-Brockman (2012) articulates with such passion and conviction, we humans must cease the pseudo reliance on a God who saves and delivers, and embrace a compassionate incarnational humanism forever reminding us that Christian salvation is about the mutual empowerment we make possible for each other following the exemplary inspiration of Jesus himself.

Thus we transcend the codependent risks of patronizing and collusive alliances, and we begin to open up possibilities for new and empowering interconnections. In recent decades, this movement has been noted in health care, counseling, and spiritual direction. Discerning the possibility (or likelihood) of a person becoming too dependent on the support of another, the client is encouraged to affiliate with support groups, thus appropriating greater self-reliance and engaging healing and wholeness through communal rather than mere individual processes.

This approach mirrors more precisely the healing and empowerment of Gospel miracles. While overtly the focus may be on individual plight or suffering, on closer examination Jesus seeks to rectify the systemic and structural forces that sustain—and may have caused—the illness in the first place. As I indicate elsewhere, Jesus' primary concern is healing rather than curing, and that healing belongs to that compassionate empowerment that welcomes and embraces all who feel excluded.

The Compassionate Interruption

In concluding her analysis of Gospel compassion, Maureen O'Connell (2009, 147) writes, "Compassion is best understood as a mystical-political interruption of self- and world-understandings that is dangerous in terms of the social upheaval it demands and promises." It is a difficult, disruptive, and uncomfortable process that sharpens first-world understandings of anthropology, suffering, and even flourishing. It requires us to see ourselves anew from the perspective of the victims of social injustice. Fresh understandings of exclusion emerge, followed by formidable challenges for more inclusive ways of perception and action.

The first interruption is perceptual and attitudinal. Our long history of Western rationality and cultural imperialism breeds a kind of superiority complex whereby we consistently relegate "the others" to an inferior marginalized status. And those who don't make it—socially, educationally, politically, and economically—are perceived to be lacking in what it takes to be authentically human. Inadvertently, we tend to judge harshly and falsely, creating an outcome whereby a huge sector of the human population is condemned to perpetual poverty, oppression, and alienation.

The second interruption evolves through a set of behaviors, mainly subconscious, whereby we tend to consign those different from ourselves to an outsider status, and set up many of the violent adversarial conflicts that have bedeviled humanity for several centuries, a violence that seems to be gaining even a deeper grip in the opening decades of the twenty-first century. We like to be with those we like, and those we don't like are not only shunned or ignored, but tend to become the focus for a range of negative projections that augment the several cultural prejudices still too common in our world and that are often reinforced by Christian churches themselves. I am alluding to the racism, ethnocentrism, religious bigotry, gender inequality, and homophobia that continue to bedevil our contemporary world.

The third interruption is institutional in nature and may be the most resistant of all to reform and renewal. How do we make the structural changes that transcend our widespread allegiance to dualistic splitting (the us versus them)? How do we re-create economic and political structures that will seek to prioritize commonalities over differences that will shift the theory of the common good into practices that engage everybody, particularly the marginalized and disenfranchised, into empowering dialogue and engagement? This cannot be achieved by our current economic strategies or by the prevailing so-called democratic political processes. The dominant economic and political systems—with their patriarchal addiction to power and domination—are too dysfunctional and preoccupied with self-perpetuation to serve the inclusive, empowering compassion of the Christian Gospel.

This brings us to the fourth disruption, and the subversive challenge of how to move forward when most, if not all, of our dominant institutions are failing dismally to deliver a truly compassionate and liberating society. Among other things, it requires the Christian to return to the Gospel and envision afresh the disruptive, subversive, empowering liberation of the parable stories. This is where Jesus provides us with the discerning wisdom to break through and transcend our crippling alienations. We will pick up this fertile trail in the next chapter.

Concluding Thought

Many times in this chapter I have drawn on Maureen O'Connell's comprehensive study on Gospel compassion. She has redeemed the concept from its often devotional and sentimental usage, and revisioned its potential for liberating and empowering solidarity, particularly for those condemned to exclusion and oppression of any kind. She summarizes her new vision and the ensuing challenges in this fourfold call to conversion (O'Connell 2009, 122):

- *A public and political commitment rather than a private and personal conviction.* Gospel compassion is not only a warm, caring feeling for somebody in pain and distress. It is an invitation to stand in the shoes of the others, feel inside not only their anguish and suffering, but viscerally entering their deep, perhaps unarticulated desire for freedom and fresh hope, and finally shifting the solidarity in the direction of the action that will change the oppressive plight in the direction of empowering liberation.

- *A dangerous participation in justice rather than a comfortable expression of charity.* A life marked with authentic compassion is a risky endeavor. It involves putting one's life on the line, transcending the comfort zone of middle-class respectability, opting for what will often be perceived as politically and religiously unacceptable.

- *An ongoing process of conversion rather than a series of unrelated acts of kindness.* It involves embracing the mind of Christ, unambiguously committed to the New Reign of God (next chapter). It means adopting and appropriating a set of values at variance with the prevailing competitive, successive-driven culture, as we desire to cocreate a world order where all can be included in a liberated and empowering way.

- *A transformative relationship between giver and receiver rather than an unreciprocated gift of self.* Gospel compassion, as Marcus Borg has highlighted, is not only another personal virtue and above all should never lead to patronizing altruism from the haves to the have-nots. It prioritizes a stance of mutual solidarity, seeking out systemic and institutional reforms so that all people— and the oppressed earth itself—can move in the direction of liberating self-realization and communal empowerment. This is inescapably a comprehensively holistic strategy that simultaneously embraces economic, political, social, and religious reform.

Chapter 4

Subversive Companionship

Jesus did not seem to care much for history. The only thing he ever wanted to do with history was change it.

— NICK PAGE

John the Baptist is often described as the forerunner to Jesus. The apocalyptic flavor of John's message can easily camouflage the subversive transformation that marked his courageous mission. The day of judgment was fast approaching, inaugurating a new age in which justice, peace, and hope would flourish. The people warmed to the message, and with hope-filled enthusiasm, many flocked to John in the desert.

However, John represented something much more basic, liberating, and empowering. The people who came to John included tax collectors, soldiers (who could have been Samaritans), and prostitutes—people who because of their very rank were deemed impure and therefore barred from temple worship. Perceptively, Nick Page (2011, 72) describes John as an antipriest: "A high priest in camel hair, waits deep in the Jordan miqvaot. His actions are priestly actions: ritual cleansing, ritual and prayer. But he did them in the wrong place and offered them to impure people." John's baptism offered an ecstatic experience of hope for those who believed they were permanently excluded; according to Nick Page (2011, 98), it included Gentiles and also quite possibly Samaritans! John was the great forerunner of radical Gospel inclusiveness.

John's activities were in direct opposition to the temple and its ideals of purity and impurity. In the wilderness, John was offering a radical alternative to the temple and its clerical imperium. John was an antiestablishment prophet. He was not hiding out in the desert, but using a liminal space to challenge and denounce the religion of exclusion. For John the temple in Jerusalem could never provide what the people needed. He was calling people to repentance, using the symbolic action of ritual bathing to embrace, include, and empower the marginalized and excluded.

Subverting Patriarchal Domination

Jesus began his missionary endeavor as a disciple of John but did not stay the course. In some aspects, Jesus seems to have opted for a vision very different from that of John, shifting the emphasis from ascetical apocalyptic doom to eschatological celebratory hope. For John, fasting was an integral dimension of the envisaged transformation, but for Jesus it was *feasting* rather than *fasting* that would deliver the new breakthrough. What Jesus did continue was the challenge to the prevailing patriarchal religiosity, taking it to new daring levels that John had not realized, and central to that expanding vision was what the Gospels describe as the Kingdom of God (Greek: *basileia*).

To appreciate the radical subversive shift—initiated by John, adopted and embellished by Jesus—we need to understand the dominant culture of the time, more accurately the power base on which life functioned and developed. It was predominantly a patriarchal value system in which males were deemed to be wiser, holier, and better able to control the destiny not only of humans, but of all creation. According to the patriarchal worldview, a male God ruled from on high, from a heavenly realm above the sky. On earth, the ruling God delegated divinely mandated authority to the king. It was the *king*—and not the priest—who served as God's primary representative on earth.

Kings inhabited royal palaces, embellished with heavenly glory. The king's palace, and not the temple, was deemed to be God's primary abode on earth, as witnessed in Solomon's thirteen-year construction of his royal palace, transcending the building of the temple by six/seven years. At the time of Jesus, the king's palace had to be nine times bigger than the temple, a guideline adopted both by Herod the Great in constructing his elaborate palace at Jerusalem, and by his son Antipas (governor from 4 to 39 CE) in the reconstruction of his fortress at Machaerus.

The kingly domain had very clear boundaries differentiating who could be in and who had to be kept outside. The majority of people never even dreamed of seeing the inside of the king's palace. And within the kings abode, rank and file mattered greatly, with strict adherence to the pecking order on the hierarchical ladder. The same ordering was mirrored in society generally, with the elite at the top and the slaves at the base. The system claimed validation from heaven itself, and like all heavenly things, it was deemed to be eternal and everlasting.

David's Paradoxical Successor

Walter Wink (2002, 250) captivates the historical climate and cultural pathos at the turn of the first Christian century when he writes,

> The world that Jesus entered was seething with human longings that showed in messianic dreams, millennial fantasies, apocalyptic desperation, mystical revelations, suicidal nationalism, religious critique and reform,

reactionary rigidity, and a sense that time was collapsing, that the future was foreshortened, that the mystery
of reality was about to be revealed. In such a milieu,
the authenticity of Jesus was like a beacon that drew all
mythological motifs to itself. Incubating in the womb of
that period was God's rash gamble that humanity might
become more humane.

The Jewish visionaries of the time anchored their hopes
in the great King David, perceived to be the archetypal liberator for the Hebrew people, a successor to whom would be the
hoped-for Messiah delivering final liberation. Even to this day, the
pre-Christmas liturgy endorses the hope invested in the Davidic
dynasty. The hoped-for Messiah would be a son of David and like
his outstanding ancestor would be endowed with royal power.
His royalty and his divinity were one and the same. God the
supreme king operated in the world primarily through kings, and
in this capacity, the king (or emperor) was perceived to be divine.

In the millennial epoch described by Walter Wink, the messianic deliverer would have to be of royal patronage. Anyone
claiming to be a Messiah but unable to establish a royal lineage
was dismissed as fraudulent. In the case of Jesus, Matthew's Gospel establishes the clear line of descent in its opening chapter
(Matt. 1:1–16). Luke follows suit in the third chapter of his Gospel (Luke 3:23–38). There are some notable differences between
the two genealogies, and their historical veracity has been extensively questioned. In reviewing those genealogies, we need to
remember that it is not history that is at stake, but validation of
divine and earthly power.

Those who believed that the historical Jesus was the promised Messiah, and son of David, postulated their belief on the fact
that he was kingly by nature and would deliver freedom through
his divine kingly power. According to Mark 1:14–15, Jesus
embarks upon his mission proclaiming a New Reign of God in

the world. The Gospels describe it as the *Kingdom of God*. It proves to be one of Christianity's most enigmatic symbols and even till the present time is the subject of intense investigation.

How the first "Christians" (crowds, disciples, scholars) interpreted the concept of the Kingdom of God we will never know for sure. The Gospels indicate that the apostles sought to enthrone Jesus as a king, something he consistently resisted. The crowds were clearly impressed by his healing and teaching, and would have assumed that he was endowed with something of the transhuman qualities of God, which culturally would be mediated through earthly kingship. The unknown variable—then and now—is the oral tradition and the language that Jesus spoke.

Jesus ministered primarily among the rural environs of Palestine. He spoke the indigenous language of his people, which was *Aramaic*, a spoken language only, and today extremely difficult to access.[1] Jesus himself wrote nothing down (in Hebrew), which means we have inherited the remnants of an oral tradition that in due course was translated into Greek, from which we have derived the Gospel texts of the present time.

Toward Empowering Kinship

Scholars suggest that the likely Aramaic word for Kingdom that Jesus adopted was *malkuta*. It carries a controversial interpretation with strong emphasis on *empowerment*, and a counterchallenge to royal dominion. As I explain in a previous work (O'Murchu 2012), I run with one popular translation: the *Companionship of Empowerment*. Something close to this understanding seems to be what the historical Jesus was trying to convey; it also describes what, in all probability, the people would have heard. (With so much royal indoctrination, we cannot be sure how well the people would have appropriated or internalized the new meaning).

The Companionship of Empowerment makes a double shift: from power over to power with, and from unilateral domination to communal collaboration (more in Crossan 2010). For purposes of the present work, it marks yet another seismic shift from exclusivity to radical inclusiveness. As in our time, so also in the time of Jesus, the royal dispensation was heavily couched in elitism and exclusion. Royal patronage was often reserved to specific families, and within the exercise of kingly power, only the privileged few obtained close access. The king's palace was heavily fortified, and admission was only allowed to a selected elite. Opulence and glory befitted royal accolade, far in excess of what the ordinary people could ever hope to experience. Between the king and the people stood a vast chasm.

It seems that the historical Jesus declared an end to such imperial exclusion, a breakthrough captivated by Wendy Farley (2011, 204) in these words: "In this empire (Kingdom of God) neither victims nor perpetrators find the door slammed in their faces. . . . If we accept its healing, we are asked to accept that everyone else in the entire world is a citizen of this Kingdom."

In the Companionship of Empowerment, the ground rule seems to be that nobody is out, and therefore everybody is considered to be included. And no longer is power and privilege reserved to the select few. The pyramid has been collapsed into a circle. Animation is activated from the center outward in an embrace that excludes no one. The "privileges" of this new dispensation belong primarily to those who have never known anything but exclusion: the poor, the marginalized, the despised, the disenfranchised. It has aptly been described as an upside-down Kingdom (Kraybill 1990).

When the confused disciples (and the Pharisees) came to Jesus and asked for clarification on this new baffling phenomenon, described in the Gospels as the "Kingdom of God," they were hoping for a clear rational answer. And that is what the surrounding Greek culture encouraged: use your reason, and always give reasonable answers. According to the Greeks at the time, that is what constituted responsible human discourse.

"So, what's the Kingdom of God all about," they queried.
"Well . . . the Kingdom may be compared to . . ." and there followed a set of stories that became more baffling by the day. And
the more the disciples queried what it was all about, the more
dislocating the stories became. Long before queer theory was
formulated by contemporary social scientists, it flourished in the
stories told by Jesus. The Gospel names them as *parables*.

Parables of Subversive Inclusivity

I leave it to the reader to sample the vast literature on parables (cf.
Dodd 1978; Herzog 1994; Crossan 1994, 2012; Levine 2014).
They share much in common with ancient precedents of every oral
culture known to humankind, yet carry subversive undercurrents
rarely found in older forms. So intriguing are these stories, it has
taken Christians some two thousand years to comprehend their
significance. And we are a long way from realizing their true depth
of meaning, one that, in fact, is likely to engage us afresh in each
new historical era and in each novel cultural context.

So let's venture straight in: *The Kingdom of God may be compared to two guys who go up to the temple to pray, one a noble
Pharisee and the other a petrified tax collector.* According the Luke
18:9–16, they both end up in an inner room of the temple!

> *First Interruption*: "Hold on a moment, tax collectors
> are ritually impure. Tax collectors oppress our people
> and should not have access to our sacred spaces. Do you
> not know your Scripture? Do you realize the dangerous
> heresy you are teaching?"

> *First Response*: "You asked me what the Kingdom is
> about. And I am telling you that in this new compan-
> ionship, there are no outsiders anymore. Everybody is
> in now, and so the guy who stood at the back (but was
> actually inside the room), beating his breast and pleading

divine mercy, he ends up more justified than the other, because in God's eyes he is no longer an outsider and must never be treated again in this way!"

Second Interruption: "That is pure heresy. We better get rid of this bastard before he wrecks our religion completely."

ও

Listen to another parable: *"There was this rich landowner, whose chief steward was reported for mismanagement. The prospect of being fired and having to resort to begging (with all the shame that went with it), scared the living daylights out of the steward. He started to use his subversive imagination, calling for swindlers like himself and swindling the books to win their good favor. In walked the landlord in the middle of one such transaction and saw right through the gerrymandering that was going on. But the mirror neurons in the landlord's brain started flashing: right in front of his eyes he saw in the steward his very own self, and he could not deny it. To the contrary, he admonished him for his ingenuity and subversive creativity for embracing in the name of love and justice the many that are cast outside."*

First interruption: "Are you suggesting that we should all become dishonest crooks?"

First response: "When you are dealing with an oppressive system, forever trying to keep people out, there are times when you play the game to your advantage! Always of course with the desire to break down the barriers of exclusion and oppression."

Second interruption: "But that is not what the Torah teaches!"

Second response: "Love God and love your neighbor. In these two is contained the whole law and the prophets as well!"

~

The parables mark a paradigm shift of rare ingenuity. They require extensive imagination, intuition, and a quality of prophetic wisdom that is truly unique. As subversive, empowering stories they have been domesticated almost beyond recognition. The Gospel writers themselves allegorize many of the parables, using them as stories to highlight the salvation wrought by Jesus over against the rejection he suffered at the hands of the Jews—an interpretation rejected by several scholars today. Others have heavily sentimentalized the parables turning them into devotional childlike stories feeding the spiritual codependency that afflicts many contemporary Christians.

The two examples I cite briefly embrace an interpretation that is more liberationist, political, and subversive in nature. These same examples make more explicit Jesus' desire to include—and empower—all those of his day who were oppressed and marginalized. I am not in any way endorsing a secular, socialistic interpretation, but rather a holistic one that breaks through all our dualistic splits between secular and sacred reality. I am regarding the parables as primordial narratives of God's desire to see nobody left outside, for any reason whatsoever!

Miracles as Parables in Action

While the parables are explicitly related to the proclamation of the New Reign of God (Kingdom), the link with the miracle stories is more subtle but, truthfully, even more subversive. Miracles yield to very challenging interpretations when we view them as *parables in action*. We have long regarded the miracles as acts of

divine intervention, whose primary purpose was to manifest the
supernatural power of the divine Jesus. This mode of understanding reinforced another dualistic split, quite alien to incarnational
wholeness, dividing the all-powerful God from the powerless
human being. Exclusion rather than inclusion was the underlying dynamic at work.

Many of the miracles are parable-type stories describing
release from *internalized oppression* arising from the debilitating impact of Roman imperialism and Jewish coercive religiosity.
Thanks to the increasingly multidisciplinary nature of biblical
studies, the oppressive nature of Roman occupation and usurpa-
tion is much better understood. It was the tax burden more than
anything else that lay heavily on people's resources, forcing them
at times to sacrifice land and property, personal security and dignity, in order to remain free of debt. Not only did it leave many
people financially impoverished, but it resulted in an unrelenting
struggle that often ensued in sickness, disability, and psychological strain, even to the point of insanity.

On top of all that was the religious taxation mainly for the
upkeep of the Temple and the financing of the priesthood itself. It
seems that the failure to meet this need often resulted in crippling
guilt, as indicated in Jesus' reassurance to the crippled man that
his sins were forgiven him (Mark 2:3–12). This seems to have
been a precondition for his restoration to normal health. In psy-
chosomatic terms, it sounds like Jesus was advising the crippled
man to first let go of the crippling impact of his guilt, as if it was
a major cause of his physical disability.

Ritual impurity seems to be another issue that often resulted
in internalized oppression, with ostracization that was more
social than medical, particularly in the case of a condition
described as leprosy. Despite the arguments of Johnathan Klawans (2005) and others that ritual purity regulations applied
mainly to the priests engaged in temple service, it does seem to
be the underlying issue in the several distinctions between in and

out that prevailed at the time. Lepers were declared unclean and barred from various types of communal association, not because of the impact on health and well-being, but because the scaling skin condition was publicly regarded as a state of impurity (for more on leprosy, see Klawans 2005, 55–57). And in this case, social and religious legalities came into play, as the person could only be pronounced clean (i.e., reintegrated into the social fabric of life) after a temple ritual, which presumably cost money.

A vivid example of a miracle as a parable in action is the story of Gerasene demoniac. The Greek text consists of many military terms, the best known being the numerical description of the demonic force—a *legion* being a cohort of possibly up to six thousand Roman foot soldiers. Is this merely a man possessed of an evil spirit, or should the "possession" be understood as a form of insanity arising from cruel, internalized oppression? Is it not likely to be some severe form of military disenfranchisement resulting in massive loss of dignity and integrity. Perhaps a savage attack resulting in the injury or death of loved ones, and the robbery of the little land he had for survival. And it does not require too much insight to realize that the pigs rushing into the sea articulates a symbolic desire to expel the Roman forces from the land of Israel.

The postcolonial reverberations of this graphic scene are well captivated by Louise Lawrence (2013, 128) when she writes, "Legion was exposed to launch a bare and filthy protest against collusion with imperial powers. Jesus' exorcism ultimately normalized this character and rendered him politically ineffective. It in turn perhaps prompted the receiver of the gospel to question the strength of Jesus' opposition to empire, or indeed expose his tacit compliance with the powers that be" (see also Lawrence 2013, 90–93).

All the miracles describe complex parables-in-action activating fresh empowerment for the many disenfranchised and ostracized. Jesus systematically waged war on everything which destroyed, distorted, cramped and enslaved human life. Whenever

Jesus finds evil in his ministry he opposes it. The movement of his life, its driving force and direction is against evil and for health, freedom, forgiveness, wholeness and fullness of life. The miracles mark a homecoming, at least in desire and aspiration, creating symbolic new thresholds for empowerment, inclusion, and fresh meaning. Disease in that culture primarily signified fragmentation of the relational web of life; the miracle story is a parable aimed at reintegration and the establishment of empowering inclusivity.

Why Did Christians Abandon the Kingdom?

The radical inclusiveness depicted in the Companionship of Empowerment, the subversive challenge of the parables, and the healing empowerment of the miracles together constitute a religious vision unique among world faith systems. Contemporary critics of religion understandably reecho Gandhi's disturbing challenge: "I like your Christ, I do not like your Christians. Your Christians are so unlike your Christ." Much of the vigor and vitality of the foundational message has been diluted and seriously subverted. As indicated elsewhere in this book, much of the betrayal happened under the corrosive influence of Constantine and legacy that proved so seductive for subsequent generations of Christians.

The Christian church(es) never lost sight of the new empowering companionship, despite being seriously compromised by church authorities. And there have been historical epochs where it flourished, albeit in subversive movements such as the Beguines of the Middle Ages and several of the nonviolent groups (e.g., Quakers, Mennonites) of later times. Not until the nineteenth century did biblical scholarship make a conscious attempt at retrieving that which had been so irresponsibly subverted.

The dualistic splitting so endemic to Christian history—and observable also in the other great religions—has also been a serious obstacle. For most of the two thousand–year history of Christianity, the Kingdom of God was deemed to be a trans-earthly, spiritual achievement, an internal disposition of the heart, a process underpinning the holy abandonment, a strategy to guarantee individual salvation—outside and beyond this vale of tears. To bolster and justify this emphasis, the statement from Luke 17:21, "The Kingdom of God is within you," was often misused and abused (see more in O'Murchu 2011, 105ff.). In this more fundamentalist understanding, the Kingdom of God belonged to the heavenly realm hereafter, not to our pilgrim engagement with the living earth.

After the more explicit retrieval of the Kingdom of God in the mid twentieth century—by Scripture scholars particularly—the pendulum swung significantly toward the social, economic, and political implications of this foundational Gospel vision. In the Catholic Church today, the split still prevails between official church teaching, as well as popular devotional practices (both of which favor a more individual spiritualized appropriation), while more progressive scholarship and a growing body of more critically minded lay believers favor the emphasis on social action.

The more informed reader will rightly retort: "But, surely, it is a both-and, rather than an either-or." The main challenge is not so much in naming the desired integration, but rather on how do we move toward the desired synthesis. Wisdom from the great mystical traditions—East and West—may be valuable here. A little known writer, Jim Marion (2000) suggests that Jesus, in his extensive employment of the term *Kingdom of God*, is invoking a nondual consciousness that does not evolve around an egoic center and does not view the world through the subject/object polarities inherent to egoic thinking. For Cynthia Bourgeault (2008, 181), the ensuing inclusivity embraces not only humans, but the entire spectrum of organic life from the human person to the vast range of cosmic organisms. She writes,

> The Kingdom of Heaven is the enlightened radiance of
> the eye that looks straight into being and sees that it is

the Body of Christ—each bird, leaf, tree; the fullness of
Being hidden in the random dots of the universe, totally
transparent to the love that is its source and its destiny.
Meaning dances within meaning; our human lives are set
ablaze to release the root energy of love, and we discover
to our amazement just how much love can be borne in
human flesh.

A Love That Empowers

The activation of such love is not a mere human accomplish-
ment, nor can it be attained by a spirituality forever seeking to
escape our earthly secular reality. Love is what makes the integration possible, and in turn the deeper synthesis is the precondition
for making the world a more lovable place. This all authenti-
cates further my suggested translation of the Kingdom of God
(Heaven) into the more Aramaic-sensitive Companionship of
Empowerment. A love that fails to empower can be a lethal trap
for oppression and conformity. It is in the process of empowering—earthlings and the living earth—that the preconditions for
a more lovable coexistence can be brought about.

Of the two terms in my suggested renaming of the Kingdom
of God, that of *companionship* is by far the more generic and
subversive. It denotes community, mutuality, cocreating together
through the mobilization of diverse gifts, as outlined in I Corinthians 12:28–31. And it also is endowed with subversive intent. It
is as if the historical Jesus wishes to transcend all forms of kingship, even benign versions, and wishes to have them all replaced
with communities for mutual empowerment. In other words,
every pyramid is to be replaced with a circle.

Nowhere is the new companionship so powerfully illustrated
than in the Jesus' last journey into Jerusalem, riding on a donkey.
Most scholars highlight possible parallels with the key Old Testament passages (1 Kings 1:33; 2 Sam. 16:2; Zech. 9:9–10). The
cultural (and geographical) symbolism may be even more poi-

gnant amid the followers who intimately knew the significance of the donkey in their rural communities for ploughing, threshing, carrying loads, and journeying. The king always rode on a *horse*, the royal beast. By choosing a *donkey*, Jesus has unambiguously collapsed the pyramid into the circle of the people going around every day with their donkeys. The exclusive power of the king on horseback gives way to the inclusive fellowship of the rank-and-file serving God, and creation, through their daily lives.

According to traditional Christianity, getting to know the mind of Christ—as suggested by Philippians 2:2—required one to become humble, long suffering, and obedient, even unto death. Surely, for our time, we must consider afresh what the mind of Christ might be as we seek to faithfully embrace the Gospel imperative: "Seek first the Kingdom of God and its justice and the rest will follow" (Matt. 6:33). If we want to know the mind of Christ, must we not engage more fully in the new companionship, embrace its vision, and live by its key values? Unfortunately, Christians have not followed that biblical imperative, and frequently the church's own collusion with royal power puts serious obstacles in the way.

Seek First . . .

It is the foundation stone of the Kingdom that evokes all the other dimensions of inclusivity explored in this book. The values of nonviolence, compassion, liberation, healing, commensality (the open table), and subversive challenge, are central to the new companionship. Not only was this the primordial vision and strategy of the historical Jesus, it is the foundational blueprint for all Christian life. It is the wellspring that must never be compromised.

All the parables ask us to imagine what the new companionship entails. It is not a subject for mere introspection and will not reveal its true meaning in any kind of rational analysis. It is not by accident that every parable opens with the word "Imagine!"

The Christian faith is imbued with a creativity that can never be expressed merely in rational prose. Walter Brueggemann (2005) claims that we cannot discern the deep meaning of the prophetic literature (in the Hebrew Scriptures) without a poetic imagination. To discern the deep truth of the Gospel—and the challenge of empowering inclusivity—we need the poetic imagination. In poetic verse, let's hear afresh the perennial call to remain ever faithful to the primacy of God's New Reign: disciples serving the Companionship of Empowerment.

Imagine a New Empowerment

Imagine a Kingdom with no king at all,
Empowering companions in charge.
Imagine the seed, the smallest by far,
Producing a tree's entourage.
Imagine a farmer his wealth to forego
To purchase a treasure so rare.
A new dispensation explodes in our midst:
Imagine . . . Imagine . . . Imagine!

Imagine a vineyard with wine flowing profuse,
The joy of a new celebration.
Imagine a banquet with no one left out,
Disrupting the known segregation.
Imagine the sower with seedlings aglow,
A harvest to relish the nations.
No more malnutrition to torture the soul;
Imagine . . . Imagine . . . Imagine!

Imagine a woman with leaven and dough
The hands that make bread to sustain us.
Imagine a table that's open to all,
Where purity laws won't estrange us.

Imagine the workers for too long subdued,
The struggle for justice is reaping.
From the least to the greatest let everyone sing:
Imagine . . . Imagine . . . Imagine!

Imagine an end to the patriarch's reign,
Collapsing the power from on high.
Imagine a circle empowering within,
A freedom so new to employ.
Imagine the demons, controlling through fear,
No longer command the high ground.
A new world order can break through at last;
Imagine . . . Imagine . . . Imagine!

Imagine the challenge disciples embrace
To model the new dispensation.
The old bureaucratic with power at its core
Lies dead in the temple's ruination.
Imagine the courage and vision we need
When the tomb of our hopes has been shattered.
And the new voice arising has another refrain:
Imagine . . . Imagine . . . Imagine!

Chapter 5

In Come the Samaritans!

*Love of the stranger as infinitely other! And wonder at
the very strangeness of it all, . . . the spiritual epiphany of
welcoming, the poetic shudder of imagining, the ethical
act of transfiguring our world by caring for the stranger
as we watch the world become sacred.*

— RICHARD KEARNEY

In the time of Jesus, the Samaritans occupied Samaria, the area
formerly known as the Kingdom of Israel. They would have
been of mixed Israelite and Arab descent, since the Assyrians
had transferred large number of Arabs and others to Samaria
after the overthrow of Israel. The Samaritans accepted the Torah
(Pentateuch) but would have nothing to do with the later books
of the Jewish Bible or with any of the new religious practices
brought back from Babylon.

According to Jewish tradition and the Bible, the modern day
Samaritans are descendants of foreign peoples who were brought
into ancient Israel after the Assyrians conquered and drove the
Judeans out in 701 BC. The Samaritans, however, trace their

ancestry to remnants of the Judean population who remained in Samaria following the conquest. Recent scholarship tends to support the Samaritan view. With the return of the Judean exiles from Babylonia in the fifth century BCE, a break developed between the Judeans and the Samaritans, resulting, in part, from the Samaritans' refusal to accept new religious texts and interpretations. At about this time, the Samaritans began calling themselves *Shomeronim* (Hebrew for "to conserve") in reference to their adherence to traditional religious beliefs and practices. Barred by the Jews from participating in the rebuilding of the Jewish temple, the Samaritans, in the fourth century BCE, built their own temple on Mount Gerizim, overlooking Nablus. The temple was destroyed in 128 BCE; a new one was built, and it too was destroyed, in 486 CE. Since the building of the first temple, Mount Gerizim has been the destination for Samaritan pilgrimages, and continued access to the site is a major concern for contemporary Samaritans.

At about the time of Jesus, the Samaritans numbered several hundred thousand and were spread in settlements across the Fertile Crescent. In late Roman times, they numbered about one million. Ever since then, their numbers and settlements steadily decreased at the hands of the Jews, Persians, Greeks, Romans, Byzantines, and Arabs. According to their own tally, there were 751 Samaritans as of January 1, 2012.

Jewish Antagonism toward Samaritans

The religious enmity between the Jews and the Samaritans dated from the return of the former from the Babylonian captivity, when the Samaritans worked to prevent the rebuilding of Jerusalem. Later they offended the Jews by extending friendly assistance to the armies of Alexander. In return for their friendship, Alexander gave the Samaritans permission to build a temple on Mount Gerizim, where they worshiped Yahweh and their tribal gods, and offered sacrifices much after the order of the temple services at Jerusalem. They continued this worship up to the time of the Maccabees, when John Hyrcanus destroyed their temple on Mount Gerizim. The Apostle Philip, in his labors for the Samaritans after the death of Jesus, held many meetings on the site of this old Samaritan temple. The antagonisms between the Jews and the Samaritans were time-honored and historic; increasingly since the days of Alexander they had had no dealings with each other.

Samaritans and Jews differed on what constituted Sacred Scripture and also on where God could best be worshipped (Mount Zion or Mount Gerazim); both sides taunted each other on these issues. However, the deeper antagonism arose from the Samaritans' alleged pagan ancestry; even to travel in Samaritan country was deemed to be polluting for Jews. Samaritans were publicly cursed in the synagogues; they could not serve as a witness in the Jewish courts; they could not be converted to Judaism; and the final blow was that in Jewish minds, they were excluded from the afterlife.

The Jews (the tribe of Judah) of Jesus' time considered the Samaritans to be no better than dogs because they felt the Samaritans had turned away from the religion of their fathers. To the Jews, the Samaritans were like traitors, and there is nothing so hated by a people as when one of their own betrays them. That's how the Jews looked at the Samaritans—as having betrayed God and their fellow Israelites.

The Samaritan Outsider on the Roadside

In the eyes of the Jews at the time of Jesus, the Samaritans were the hated outsiders. And the further out they could be kept, the better. When it comes to Gospel lore, the Samaritans emerge as the great boundary breakers. Allegedly it was not safe for anybody to travel through their territory, yet Jesus occasionally did so (cf. Luke 9:51-62; 17:11; John 4:4). For Jesus, it seems they were not hated outsiders; to the contrary, they became the catalysts of some of the most vivid stories of inclusivity recorded in the Gospels.

Three stories stand out in bold relief, illustrating unambiguously cultural and religious transgression. Queer theory could scarcely do better than this. In steps the Samaritan, and we have to wrestle with inclusive transgression on a truly provocative scale. The outstanding stories include those of the Good Samaritan (Luke 10:25–37), the woman at the Well (John 4:1–40), the leper who gave thanks (Luke 17:11–19). And paradoxically, it is Jesus himself who catalyzes the subversive breakthrough. It is not only a case of bringing in the Samaritan outsider; rather it is the Samaritan outsider who unlocks the gates through which divine liberation cascades like a mighty flood.

The story of the Good Samaritan (Luke 10:25–37) is the best known of these subversive parabolic stories. We need to remember that the description of being *half dead* translates into being ritually impure. Consequently, the priest and the Levite, striving to be ever faithful to their religion—the same religion as that of the historical Jesus—walk on the other side of the road, to make sure they do not become ritually contaminated.

From the beginning, the message is loud and clear: irrespective of his cultural or religious condition, this man must be included. In the Companionship of Empowerment there are *no* outsiders! There were several options open to Jesus to declare the vision of radical inclusiveness, yet, he chose a radical outsider to be the primary catalyst. He chose *a Samaritan*! This was probably the greatest insult Jesus could have hurled at his own people, a riposte to the honor-shame dynamic that would have even deeply disturbed his own followers.

First, the Samaritan becomes the inclusive hero. He spares nothing in his act of inclusion, devoting extensive time and unlimited financial resources to ensure the suffering man was given the best of treatment. The outsider becomes the model disciple for the new companionship.

Second, there is the subtle message, which is even more provocative. By adopting the Samaritan as the hero of the story,

Jesus himself is embracing and endorsing such exemplary subversive discipleship. The one who questions the status quo—political and religious—and effectively ridicules the religious establishment must also be embraced in the circle of radical inclusiveness. It is important to note that in all these parabolic situations, Jesus transgresses normative Jewish faith and culture on a massive scale, yet he never apologizes for doing so, nor does he ever attempt to explain his reasons or reassure those who might be offended by his behavior. In this new Companionship of Empowerment, subversives belong within and must not be kept outside.

In these parabolic stories we are dealing with what Walter Brueggemann names as the prophetic imagination, and to exercise such imaginative breakthroughs we will often need more creative articulations such as poetry, art, dance, music, etc. I find poetry particularly powerful to unlock the prophetic and subversive undercurrents in the parable under consideration.

The Jericho Road Full of Questions

Every bone in my body was aching,
And a gash just below my left eye
Left me dazed with confusion and anger,
One more victim as crime rates soar high!
I had heard many stories and warnings,
That road should not travel alone.
But I thought I was fit and impervious
A lesson too late to bemoan!

Many passed me and stared in amazement,
I never felt so much betrayed,
As I glimpsed the far priest and the Levite
My stomach it groaned in despair.
Till a guy with a donkey approached me,

A stranger so thoughtful and rare.
And he mounted me on to his donkey
And rushed me for medical care.

Next, I knew I was sleeping in comfort
And sustained with some food of the best.
But in nervous concern I queried
What 'twould cost me to be such a guest.
No worry but trust in the carer,
Had accounted for every expense,
With such care I could quickly recover
And no one would ask recompense.

But then came the shock and the quandary.
O Dear! How it made my heart sink!
Compromising my whole reputation,
Betraying my unique Jewish rank.
Samaritans we always have hated,
For me they're the lowest of low.
How disgusting—he handled my body,
I better let nobody know!

But why did he do this good turn?
Now surely he too must have known
That Jews and Samaritans differ
And should keep far apart on their own.
I'm confused and unsure of my grounding,
I don't understand what's going on.
While the Jews all passed by and ignored me,
A Samaritan lifted my hand!

Who said we should hate all who differ?
On our own we should only rely?
And why is religion so righteous

Leaving people like me in the mire?
The Samaritans I still do not like them.
After all, I've been told that from youth.
But I can't trust the Jews any longer
'Cos I doubt if they're telling the truth.

And I wonder about all this religion,
Is it leading God's people astray?
When the outcast can glow in compassion
While the righteous pile rules to obey!

The Samaritan Woman at the Well (John 4:1–40

This is a great favorite among retreat-givers and a cherished text for prayer and meditation. The problem with these more spiritualized expressions is that they often short circuit the prophetic dimension with its radical, social, and political boundary breaking.

Perhaps the story should be described as a parable with many of the parabolic features of shock, expansion, transgression, disorientation. We are told that the disciples had gone into the city (Sychar) to buy food (v. 7). Normally, Jews did not eat food that was produced or handled by Samaritans. In fact, the rabbis had denounced such behavior, suggesting that eating food produced by Samaritans was the equivalent of eating swine's flesh. Why are the disciples transgressing social and religious expectations? Is the vision of the inclusive open table already captivating their souls?

A woman of Samaria comes to draw water. This intimates her poverty, suggesting that she had no servant to draw the water. For a rabbi to be alone with a woman was a social taboo, all the more transgressive when it turns out to be a woman perceived to be ethnically inferior and socially immoral.

Jesus then did something even more transgressive: he spoke to a woman in public and worse still to a Samaritan woman. Jesus asked her for a drink of water. She was understandably shocked: why was a Jewish man speaking to her, a Samaritan woman? He also should not have wanted to share a vessel with her for drinking water since it would be considered unclean. Understandably, she was baffled and confused.

Then begins an intriguing conversation full of subtlety and subversive undercurrent. Firstly the woman recognizes the societal barriers and boundaries that keep her in her place (v. 9) but at the same time she challenges Jesus' authority over and against the ancestors of her faith (4:12). Like Nicodemus, she first interprets Jesus' words on a literal level, but explores what Jesus has to offer rather than question the possibility (v. 15). Who is leading the conversation here, Jesus or the woman? Despite her lowly status, and perceived ethnic inferiority, is this not a woman engaging in a sophisticated theological conversation, and basically setting the pace (cf. Spina 2006, 151–52)? In our desire to honor the primacy of faith in Jesus, and in our regard for Jesus as the primary focus of faith, do we not run the risk of underestimating and subverting the prophetic role of the Samaritan woman?

The Samaritans believed there was no prophet after Moses, except the one of whom the great Hebrew leader had spoken— "a prophet like unto me" (Deut.18:15ff.)—whom they identified with the Messiah. It sounds like the woman at the well is striving to discern if Jesus could possibly be the Messiah. First, she switches the conversation toward the topic of worship. And here comes another inclusive bombshell! Why reduce worship to a specific religion, culture, or place? Why can't worship consist of celebrating a common spiritual heritage, potentially shared by all, and transcending all the denominational boundaries that are no longer needed? That was certainly a revolutionary idea and potentially more explosive than the transgression of strained relationships between Jews and Samaritans.

Second, we come to the notion of the five husbands (vv. 16–18), the subject of sustained moralistic rhetoric, even by some scholars who advocate that a symbolic interpretation of John's Gospel should always be prioritized. One possibility is that she was unable to have children; she was barren. So it is possible that the men who had married her then found out that she couldn't have children and opted to divorce her in order to marry more fertile women. She could also be trapped by the Levirate marriage law. Her five husbands could have been brothers for whom she was supposed to produce an heir (cf. Matt. 22:24–28). Either the family ran out of sons or the next son could have refused to marry her. That she was living with a man now who was not her husband could have been the lesser of two evils. Since the culture provided economic security only within family structures, her only other choice after husband number five died (or divorced her) might have been prostitution.

I am keeping with the oft-noted tendency in John's Gospel to adopt symbolic language over literal narrative; we need to seek out other lines of inquiry for the significance of the five husbands. In the political history, Samaria has had five foreign gods since the occupation by the Assyrians (see 2 Kings 17:30–31), and the one the Samaritans worship now is not Yahweh, but the Roman emperor. In this case, husbands should be translated as gods or lords. Supporting this interpretation, Sandra Schneiders (1999, 190, 195) asks that we adopt an adultery/idolatry metaphor rather than a literal interpretation of the five husbands. Instead we need to view the Samaritan woman not as a sinner but as a woman theologian, trying to discover her deepest truth, looking for acceptance, love, and trust, rejecting that which fails to satisfy and engaging Jesus in a theological debate about what true worship really means:

> Nowhere in the fourth Gospel is there a dialogue of such theological depth and intensity. Jesus' conversation with Nicodemus in chapter three ends with a long theological monologue by Jesus in which Nicodemus has ceased to participate. . . . The woman is not simply a "foil" feeding Jesus cue lines. She is a genuine theological dialogue partner. (Schneiders, 1999, 191)

Finally, she leaves the water jar and returns to her people informing them of her prophetic encounter and her new-found wisdom. We are told that many believe because of her commendation. But there is an exclusionary misogynist twist at the very end of the narrative (v. 42): "We don't believe because you, a woman, has convinced us. We have checked him out for ourselves, and we choose to believe on our on conviction, and not simply on the basis of your worlds." Misogyny dies slowly!

In the spirit of this amazing narrative of such empowering liberation, let's give the Samaritan woman the last word, and let poetic imagination render her the justice she deserves:

Welling-up with Samaritan Wisdom

The Samaritan woman they greet me,
Please call me Photini by name.
And I relish my place at the wellsprings
Contributing to Jacob's fame.
This country of mine is Samaria,
Long hated in biblical lore.
But our parable fame is impressive,
The truth we convey is decisive,
And the wisdom we hold is excessive
For the hearts that discern the truth.
So probe the recesses of Wisdom
And literalize not the facts.
'Cause the Gospel of John is symbolic;
Often truth is revealed in the cracks.

We broke all the laws of the Scripture
By sharing a vessel to drink
And a rabbi alone with a woman
Was another infringement to link.
Transgressing our ethnic distinctions

We chose to build bridges anew.
While birthing a wisdom transgressive,
Our dialogue was deep and impressive,
And we theologized quite excessive
Which the Gospel of John fails to note.
It clings to the male at the forefront
With me in a secondary role,
But in fact it was I did the pacing
Empowering a dialogue so whole.

I welcomed his bold invitation
To outgrow the worship we knew
Transcending the mountain and city
In the power of the Spirit's fresh hue.
My five metaphorical husbands
The Gospel of John misconstrues.
Five rulers immersed in corruption,
My country in sacred disruption,
Crying out for true liberty's option
A marriage bond yet to be sealed.
It had nothing to do with my personal fate
As moralists like to impute.
Our dialogue was cued to a symbolic depth,
Towards the dream of another repute.

A people so battered and shattered in fate
Found it hard to accept my new vision.
They would rather I drew the water in haste
And abide by my servile condition.
But I knew I'd encountered a wisdom so rare
The freedom and hope we had dreamed for.
They flocked to the source of freedom to see,
They checked for themselves the truth of my plea,
And they basked in the promise of a new liberty

With a strangely misogynist twist!
For the Gospel of John distorts to negate
What I as a woman had birthed.
"We have heard him ourselves, get out of the way,
We'll trust only what we've contested."

Despite the rejection and the hurt set aflame,
Despite the description, ignoring my name,
Some day we might re-write what's been misconstrued
Round the well of true wisdom where truth can't be fooled.
(Originally published in O'Murchu 2011, 117–19)

The Leper Who Gave Thanks (Luke 17:11-19)

Leprosy was an affliction that represented uncleanliness. It was a skin condition, which manifested as white patches on the skin, running sores, and the loss of parts of the body that became necrotic. Much worse was the social castigation that accompanied the condition, the debilitating nature of which is elucidated by Louise Lawrence (2013, 87ff.). Leprosy was regarded as one of the more obnoxious forms of ritual impurity. A leper became a total outcast within his own community. He could not enter the temple and not even a walled city; and he could not come near a Jew, much less touch one. Someone who came close to him or touched him would be considered unclean, until he fulfilled various ceremonies prescribed in the law. A leper was truly an exile among his own people.

It's important to note that the leper asks to be cleansed, not cured. Therefore the healing is not only the restoration of physical well-being, but more significantly reclaiming his legitimate place in the cultural web of relationships. His plea was that he be allowed to become a normal human being once more and could now be the recipient of acceptance, love, and social approval.

Sending the leper to the priest initially sounds strange, since Jesus clearly contested much of what the priesthood represented.

Leviticus 14 spells out, at great length, the ceremonial cleansing facilitated by the priest. In the case of Jesus and the healed lepers the sending to the priest may require a number of explanations to highlight various nuances of meaning. The priest could not make a leper well or clean. He only did diagnoses and then informed everyone whether the person in question was clean or unclean.

In terms of the present narrative, the cleansed leper goes to the priest. If the priest declares him ritually pure, then the priest is unwittingly confirming the power of Jesus to cleanse a leper. By declaring him clean, he was giving expert witness to the authenticity of the miracle. Paradoxically, therefore, the law of Moses (through this priest) was testifying to Jesus. Might this not be the significance of the phrase "As a testimony to them" (Mark 1:44)? The certification of his cleansing by the priest was the necessary testimony to the people that he was indeed cleansed and could return to living a normal life with his family and friends. But is it not also a testimony to the healer, whose compassionate mercy and healing empowerment has facilitated the man's reentry into full fellowship with his community?

It may not be a case of Jesus affirming the sacrificial system of the Jews, nor necessarily collusion with the oppressive demands for ritual purity. In a paradoxical way, Jesus embraces the system, while at the same time undermining its ideological grip on people's value and dignity. Why worry about dismantling the clericalized system, when it becomes clear that a greater force for wholeness is at work!

Furthermore, there seems to be a subversive twist to this story, often bypassed by commentators. In Mark 1:41, we are told that Jesus was moved with *pity*. According to Maurice Casey (2010, 63), the original Aramaic source is likely to have offered a different interpretation, which some Greek sources translate as *orgistheis* (meaning *being angry*), while others altered it to *splanchnisttheis* (*having compassion*), the translation adapted by both Matthew and Luke.[1] An original Aramaic word, *regaz*, is best translated as trembling with anger and deeply moved.

What was Jesus angry about? The oppression, the exclusion, the degradation lepers had to endure? And what about the temple priests reinforcing their power and control at the expense of the plight of the oppressed and marginalized—was that the focus of Jesus' anger? We can never be sure why Jesus was angry, but his passion for justice, inclusion, and empowerment certainly becomes more transparent and credible by adopting that uncomfortable translation. And while we cannot resolve the linguistic complexity, poetry helps to express something of the deep emotion underpinning the desire for a more inclusive and empowering sense of justice.

In Comes the Samaritan Leper

It's the story of a leper who's once again made whole
While the narrative itself is rendered weak.
The limits of translation usurp subversive speech
And the healing for empowerment is covertly oblique.
Was Jesus moved by "pity" or the" pathos" that empowers?
The verb of righteous anger, the exclusion that devours.
The one who touched the leper himself becomes unclean.
As the plot begins to thicken,
At a pace that's sure to quicken
The old familiar world is shaken to the core.

The healing and the wholeness is amplified in scope
With the leper representing the millions without hope.
And the laws and regulations, the ritual and the code,
Destabilized forever, leading systems to implode.
And did Jesus tell the leper to comply with priestly norm?
And the cleansing wrought by Moses to which he should
        conform?

Deprive we not the parable the author undermined.
The healing is symbolic,
The story parabolic,
Betray we not the prophet who had other things in mind.

Obeying the law of Moses would impress respected folks,
But subversiveness has little time for that.
Companions for empowerment, a much more urgent task,
Bringing freedom from oppression and justice that will last.
The town they may not enter, imperial control,
But the countryside's receptive to all who want to know.
The fertile re-awakening, with healing to empower.
We sow the seeds for justice
With healing and forgiveness,
Proclaiming unashamedly the power of God's new hour.

Finally, we come to the explicit point of the story: *the grati-tude of the Samaritan.* The Samaritan was the only one to give thanks, a gesture usually aligned with his Gentile status, thus highlighting the lack of gratitude among the Jews (the other nine) who failed to welcome and follow Jesus as Messiah. By adopt-ing this anti-Jewish polemic, we run the risk of ignoring more fertile meaning. The failure of the other nine to relish gratefully in the new empowering healing and inclusivity may have arisen from religious influence but could equally be a response aris-ing from the awesome liberation of this breakthrough, just as those in the Gerasene territory who witnessed the liberation of the demoniac asked Jesus (and the healed man) to leave their territory. The daunting challenge of now having to include and embrace so many, who formerly were barred and excluded, was just too much for many folk. The imperative of Gospel inclusivity requires a deep change of heart and spirit.

And there is the empowering corollary of the inclusivity itself, the underlying potency of unconditional love. When the outsider becomes empowered by being included, then there is a distinctive likelihood that the one-time outsider now becomes the catalyst to foster the new liberation to a degree that exceeds even conventional disciples. Is the gratitude of the tenth leper merely a description of appreciation, or is it a proactive gesture of discipleship with an intensity exceeding the normal expectations of Gospel following? Is the gratitude not a statement of wanting to give all, with unlimited love and generosity of heart?

Chapter 6

The Inclusive Table

Jesus welcomed these outcasts into table fellowship with himself in the name of the Kingdom of God, . . . It is hard to imagine anything more offensive to Jewish sensibilities.

— NORMAN PERRIN

The meals of early Christianity offered social practice at trust, imagination, and freedom.

— HAL TAUSSIG

Of all the transgressions recorded in the Christian Gospels, Jesus' indulgent feasting at table shows blatant disregard for prevailing norms. Here, inclusion is pushed to unprecedented limits, in a culture where distinctions pertaining to table etiquette carried unquestioned significance.

This is a topic that has been extensively researched in recent times, with fine overviews by Dennis E. Smith (2003), and Hal Taussig (2009). Combining historical and cultural insights backed up by archeological and sociological evidence, we have some quite detailed analyses of how food was shared in a range of different ritual and social contexts. The best known of the public meals were those of the symposium described in detail by modern researchers of which Dennis Smith (2003) is one of the better-known exponents.

The symposium was an organization of all-male groups, aristocratic and egalitarian at the same time, which affirm their identity through ceremonialized drinking. Prolonged drinking followed the meal proper. There is wine mixed in a krater for equal distribution. The participants, adorned with wreaths, lay on couches. The symposium had private, political, and cultural dimensions, reassuring the aristocrats they enjoyed social control of the polis (city). Music, poetry, and other forms of entertainment ensued, bound up with a range of liberal sexual practices. Despite what to moderns might seem like moral laxity, the symposium was perceived as the epitome of patriarchal order: there were prescribed courses of food as well as of talk. Thus the mouth was regulated as to what and when certain things were eaten and drunk as well as to what was said. The symposium communicated order, not chaos (cf. Plutarch, *Table Talk* 1.2, 616, A–B) and so involved explicit and implicit rules of decorum.

The diligence and vigilance of getting it right are all too obvious. With such a clear view of what was expected from the participants, and the various boundaries they were meant to maintain—especially in terms of who was allowed in and who would be kept outside—we can glean how disruptive and shocking it must have been to experience the new transgressive conviviality that Jesus introduced.

The Culture of Table Fellowship

Jerome Neyrey (1996) provides a valuable contextual overview of the prevailing norms and expectations around table fellowship at the time of the historical Jesus. He outlines a schema of mapping out both structures and expectations related to who eats with whom, what is eaten, where, when, how.

1. *Maps of Persons.* Who eats with whom? Likes eat with
    likes; family eats with family, Pharisees with Pharisees.
    Secondly, there are maps of where people sit at a meal
    (e.g., Philo, *Contemplative Life* 67, 69, 75; Plutarch,
    Table Talk 1.3; Luke 14:7–11). Seating arrangements
    signify and replicate one's role and status in a group,
    its order and hierarchy. We speak of a "head" table at
    a banquet; the host sits at the head place (see Plutarch,
    Table Talk 1.2). His "right hand" is traditionally the
    place of honor (Luke 20:42; Acts 2:33).

    Greco-Roman and Jewish meals owe much of their
    structure to a more formal meal known as the sympo-
    sium, at which there were elaborate maps of persons.
    Roles are clearly specified: a host, a chief guest, and
    other guests. Places taken by the participants reflect their
    status, with the chief guest closest to the host and the
    other guests arranged in some declining order of impor-
    tance.

2. *Map of Things.* Certain foods were proscribed and oth-
    ers prescribed. Jews had an elaborate code of clean and
    unclean foods. According to the Jewish Torah, we note
    the following three guidelines: (a) the meat of certain
    animals was considered unfit for table (Lev. 11; Deut.
    14); (b) of those admitted as edible, blood had to be sep-
    arated from the meat before cooking (Lev. 17:10; Deut.
    12:23–27); and (c) there had to be a total separation of
    milk from meat, which involves the minute specializa-
    tion of utensils (Exod. 23:19, 34:26; Deut. 14:21). These
    kosher concerns extended even to the dishes used in the
    preparation and consumption of foods, for example,
    Pharisaic concern for the porosity of vessels and their
    ritual washing. The conversation at table is also mapped.
    Certain talk is appropriate and even required at meals.
    At a Passover meal, specific benedictions for each of the

four cups are pronounced, as well as the recitation of the
Exodus haggadic and the Hallel psalms.

3. *Maps of Places.* The symbolic order of the universe is
   replicated in the spatial arrangement of persons and
   things at a meal and in regard to the locale where one
   sits (e.g., dining room or temple precinct). A Pharisee, for
   example, would concern himself with the place where
   he ate to ensure that the proper diet was prepared in
   the way that safeguarded matters of ritual purity, further
   guaranteed by serving the food with proper utensils.

4. *Maps of Times.* Although daily meals vary in terms of
   frequency and time of day, formal meals reflect a serious concern for proper time and sequencing. Considerable attention was paid to the exact time when Shabbat
   started to determine when to begin the weekly Shabbat
   meal. Even in the course of a meal, we find elaborate
   time arrangements according to which dishes are served
   in a fixed sequence.

Obviously, we know a great deal more about public ceremonial meals, such as banquets (symposia), funerary meals, and
those specifically related to religious feasts such as Passover. At
such gatherings, the meal reflected the symbolic system of the
surrounding culture. In fact, the meal served as a kind of window
through which to view the symbolic universe of the time. Family meals at home would be conducted with less formality and
much more spontaneity. Nonetheless to lesser or greater degree,
the following guidelines loomed in the background:

Who: who eats with whom; who sits where; who per-
forms what action; who presides over the meal;
What: what is eaten (or not eaten); how it is tithed (pur-
chased), or grown or prepared; what utensils are used;
what rites accompany the meal (e.g., washing of hands

or full bath); what is said (as well as the observance of silence);

When: when one eats (daily, weekly, etc.; time of day); when one eats what is the order and timing of the various courses;

Where: where one eats (room); where one sits; in which institution (family, politics);

How: how one eats, at a table or not; sitting, standing or reclining.

Ritual Purity and Table Etiquette

Scholars differ in their understanding of ritual cleanliness at the time of Jesus (see the detailed overview in Meier 2009, 342ff.). The majority consider it to be quite a substantial issue, clearly a prerogative for the Pharisees and for the temple priests. Observance among rank-and-file Galileans is thought to be less rigorous. However, we can assume that anybody seeking to be more religiously devout and zealous would endeavor to maintain as high a standard as possible in terms of all the legal expectations related to Torah observance.

The first key characteristic of the meal, as practiced by the Pharisees, is the strict regulations surrounding what foods were allowed and what was prohibited. They ate only those foods that were approved by the Mosaic law and took great pains to ensure that even that food did not become corrupt through contact with any unclean vessel or person. This reflects their view that they were a chosen people—a privilege zealously guarded in every detail of behavior, including what could and could not be eaten.

In addition to the food itself, many Jewish groups had strict regulations surrounding who should and should not be included in the dinner meals for religious reasons. For example, the Qumran documents prohibit any Gentiles, women, or those with physical defects from eating with the company (and in the home, a menstruating woman always ate in isolation from the rest of the family). This type of practice is also seen in the Pharisees as portrayed by Luke, as there are many disputes over the people with whom Jesus eats. The Pharisees, in their concern for purity, attempted to replicate the purity and practices of the temple on a household level. Even for those included by the Pharisees and other groups, however, there was jockeying for social position (Luke 14:7–11). One's place at the table was reflective of one's position in the society, and so the table fellowship was a source of contention as each one tried to establish a higher place in the order and structure of the society.

A second significant feature of table fellowship was how people were perceived and judged in terms of their relationship with God. Upholding purity regulations was a perceived requirement for religious fidelity. Some people, for reasons of ethnicity or economic and social standing, automatically were excluded from participating in the meal, which symbolically reflects their exclusion both from the temple and the possibility of attaining full membership in the people of God.

Thus there follows the third key element: those of a certain economic status were considered blessed by God in their wealth and therefore considered only their own type as suitable companions at the common table. The poor stayed with the poor and the rich with the rich. In this way, the economic classes were stratified, and the facility for reciprocity was streamlined as the Norwegian scholar, Halvor Moxnes indicates. In terms of the table fellowship, Moxnes (1987, 158–67) outlines three possible forms of reciprocity: negative, balanced, or vaguely generalized. Negative reciprocity is the attempt to get something for nothing; it is the attempt to take advantage of someone for one's own gain. Balanced reciprocity is the practice of mutual exchange in an attempt to maintain a good social relationship. Generalized reciprocity is giving without expectation of reciprocity or return for what one has given. The typical relationship in first-century

Palestine was one of balanced reciprocity as practiced by the upper economic classes of the people. Among the wealthy, one would engage in meals of hospitality only if one could be sure that the gesture of friendship and hospitality would be repaid. But Jesus abolishes the expected balanced reciprocity when he says, "You will be blessed, *because they cannot repay you*. You will be repaid at the resurrection of the just" (Luke 14:14).

Gospel Commensality

Paradoxically, it is our Christian devotion to the Eucharist that seriously jeopardizes the subversive inclusivity of Gospel food sharing. We place so much emphasis on the Last Supper—and its exclusive nature with allegedly only the twelve apostles present—that we do a grave injustice to the egalitarian practice of Gospel commensality and Jesus' unambiguous love for the open table.

For much of Christendom—and even till the present time—we describe the ministry of the historical Jesus in terms of his preaching and teaching. We highlight his rabbi-style evangelism above all else. Presumably we do this at a conscious level in our desire to honor the Jewishness of Jesus, while often underestimating the subconscious validation it provides for our own patriarchal need to dominate and control. Scripture scholar John Dominic Crossan (1991) proposes a very different starting point. He suggests that it would have been the healing and commensality (the common table) that most deeply touched and transformed those who first encountered the living Jesus. Through the healing and participation in the open table people were healed, affirmed, and empowered; they became the recipients of incarnational transformation.

We easily forget that Jesus was primarily about empowerment, with a radical option for the kind of inclusivity explored in the present work. Those values were realized primarily in the experiential embrace of healing and table fellowship. The preaching and teaching made greater sense after people had experienced the liberation and empowerment of inclusive fellowship. What that experience felt like is succinctly captivated by Fran Ferder and John Heagle (2002, 159–60) in the following quote:

> Meals are the most frequent setting for Gospel stories. They range from informal picnics on hillsides to banquets given by dignitaries. They introduce us to some of the most diverse and colorful of Gospel characters: a woman with long hair who washes Jesus' feet, a little boy who has loaves and fishes hidden in the folds of his robe, and a short man, named Zacchaeus, who is about to have an unexpected dinner guest. Meals transport us from a wedding in Cana to a quiet dinner at a little house in Emmaus. They invite us to a party for a prodigal and let us share a Passover supper with a carpenter's son.
>
> Meals also function as a context for the central themes of the Gospels—abundance, forgiveness, respect, compassion, love. Here, as the centerpiece of Luke's Gospel, the dinner at the Pharisee's house brings all these topics together in a lesson about who is welcome at our tables.
>
> This theme of inclusivity is one of the benchmarks of Jesus' teaching. Everyone ought to have a place at the table, especially those who have been marginalized. Obviously, this includes many who do not quality from the guest list—people who have been relegated to the back roads and slums of the towns. When we give a luncheon, we need to make sure than no one who wants to be there is left out. Inclusivity is a Gospel mandate. It is not separate from Sabbath observance, but a central part of it.

Clearly Jesus loved food and seems to have seized every possible opportunity for a party and feast with all who were willing to throw caution to the wind and join in the nourishing revelry.

And Jesus would probably be quite shocked by the degree to which the Christian church throughout the ages has invoked his name to justify fasting and an ascetical approach to food. For the historical Jesus it was feasting, and not fasting, that marked his celebratory empowering praxis.

New Testament Meals

Our understanding of New Testament meals has been quite distorted by the inflated emphasis on the Last Supper (cf. Humphreys 2011), creating a widespread impression that (1) it was distinctly different from all other meals; (2) it was exclusively for the twelve apostles only; (3) it has a more direct bearing on our salvation as a Christian people; and (4) it provides the central Gospel foundation for the Christian Eucharist. All the other Gospel meals are relegated to an inferior, secondary importance.

Commentators often fail to highlight the fact that all the other meals were inclusive, empowering, and unambiguously perceived by the historical Jesus as central to that transformed way of life we describe as redemptive or salvific. Moreover, for many years now, Scripture scholars disapprove of the practice of isolating specific passages or stories as "'proof texts'" for doctrinal truth. A more responsible mode of discernment requires us to employ all the relevant texts and stories, and not specially selected ones, often adopted for spurious imperial intent (e.g., using the Last Supper as evidence for an exclusive male priesthood).

Nick Page (2011, 245) captivates the inclusive originality and the egalitarian consequences of the Last Supper in an inspiring passage:

> After that comes the meal. Proper messiahs would have had a victory banquet. Jesus had bread and wine: the universal foods of the Greco-Roman world. The sound of the mill stones and the smell of baking filled the streets of every city, town and village. Equally, vineyards

were everywhere on the hillsides and in the villages; even
in the city we may assume that vines were grown, effectively forming roofs along some of the narrower streets.
There was nothing exotic about this feast . . . Just a cup,
bread and wine. A simple prophesy of what is to come,
and a celebration which would spread around the world.

In prioritizing New Testament commensality I want to highlight a Gospel story that might aptly be described as a parable
for commensality.

Jesus said to them, "Which of you, if you go to a friend
at midnight, and tell him, 'Friend, lend me three loaves
of bread, for a friend of mine has come to me from a
journey, and I have nothing to set before him,' and he
from within will answer and say, 'Don't bother me. The
door is now shut, and my children are with me in bed.
I can't get up and give it to you'? I tell you, although he
will not rise and give it to him because he is his friend,
yet because of his persistence, he will get up and give
him as many as he needs." (Luke 11:5–8)

Luke allegorizes this parable, using it as a rationale for persistent prayer. In its foundational meaning, this is a parable about
hospitality, one that gets us right to the heart of the commensality
described above. In Palestine of Jesus' time, people often pre-
ferred to travel after dark in order to avoid the heat, and it was
not uncommon for visitors to arrive unannounced.

No matter what time of day or night one arrives, the Jewish
norms of hospitality require that you attend to the person's need
(Gen. 18:1–8; Heb. 13:2). There is no question of refusing. For a
host to be unable to offer hospitality to a guest would be shameful; more importantly, it would bring shame not only on himself,
but upon the entire village. A guest is a guest of the community,
not just of the individual, and to comply with the cultural (and

religious) expectations, a guest must leave the village with a good feeling about the hospitality offered not just by individuals, but by the village-as-community.

At night, food may not be as readily available, since bread was baked in the morning to meet each day's anticipated needs. Despite the practical difficulties, the village hospitality demands that bread must be provided for the guest. So, the host decides to walk to his neighbor's house, knock on his door, and ask him for three loaves of bread. This householder is also bound by the expectations of cultural hospitality, and despite the great inconvenience, he gets up and gives bread for the traveler.

Various commentators strive to discern what the parable states about God's hospitality to those who cry out in need. And several critical assessments have been made of the Greek word *anaideian,* translated as "shamelessness" or "importunity" in Luke 11:8. It strikes me that this is first and foremost a parable of Gospel commensality stating unambiguously that

1. There is no room for any form of exclusion in Christian discipleship;
2. Hospitality is a primary means through which Christian inclusivity is made possible;
3. Central to such hospitality is the sharing of food;
4. In exercising such inclusivity, the person and the village share an interdependent mutual accountability; and
5. This is what God desires for all humans, and that is what humans must never deny to one another.

The Inclusive Empowerment of the Holy Spirit

Another key text is that of Luke 24:13–35, popularly known as the Emmaus story. Several subplots are intertwined in this parabolic narrative. Of specific concern for the present chapter is the culmination to the story in which Jesus leads the disillusioned two people to the table of shared commensality. There their fears are finally resolved as they recognize him in the breaking of the bread. Here we are dealing with a form of recognition far beyond normal human recognition. And the mystical clue is in Luke 24:31: "And their eyes were opened and they recognized him; and he vanished from their sight."

Where did Jesus vanish to? Seldom has the question been asked, and rarely has an answer been attempted. In classical parabolic engagement, we must move in the power of creative imagination and strive to follow where the Spirit will lead. In rational terms, we can surmise that Jesus vanishes back into his resurrected state (whatever exactly that was) or that he vanished back to the Father. All that is too rational and logical for parabolic wisdom. How about opting for an inward rather than an outward vanishing? And what might it mean if we follow the mystical logic of Jesus vanishing into the group and not out from them?

In theological terms, we are moving from Christology to Pneumatology. One of the oldest theological understandings of Eucharist is structured around the invocation of the Holy Spirit, popularly known by the Latin word, *Epiclesis*. It literally means *invocation*, the calling down of the Holy Spirit to transform the ordinary gifts of bread and wine into the sacred food of the Eucharistic celebration. The Christian churches have long debated the change brought about in the course of the Eucharistic liturgy, using terms such as *transfiguration, trans-signification, transubstantiation*. In all cases, the popular understanding is that change is activated through the power of the priest pronouncing the words of consecration over the elements. That is not the understanding conveyed in the adoption of the Epiclesis; here is an unambiguous statement that change is activated through the invocation of the Holy Spirit. The Holy Spirit and not the priest is the primary catalyst for empowering change in every Eucharistic celebration.

Several complex theological issues arise at this juncture, beyond the remit of the present work. Suffice to highlight the fact that in Christian faith, the Holy Spirit is the energizing agent in all growth and transformation, including that of the divine life communicated through the sacraments, in this case through the Eucharist.[1] And that divine desire to nourish and sustain, in the gracious generosity of the one we call Holy Spirit of God, should never be restricted to a select group, Christian or otherwise. The energizing Spirit makes the sun to shine on all in the empowering process of photosynthesis, through which the creative divine energy flows into the cosmic and planetary web of life, and into humans through the nourishing potential of daily food. It is that nourishing miracle that we celebrate in Eucharist, an earth feast to which all are invited as full participants in the empowering call of the Eucharistic Epiclesis (invocation).

When the Gospels tell us that Jesus gathered sinners, tax collectors, and prostitutes around the table of fellowship, it was not mere charity or a patronizing gesture of good will. It was a highly subversive and empowering gesture by one who himself was ever faithful to God's Holy Spirit. The commensality provided a forum to tell painful stories and dream utopian hopes. The basic affirmation of being acknowledged, accepted, welcomed, encouraged, and supported to make a fresh start were all in place. These meals were particularly groundbreaking by including women as full and equal members—even women of questionable character. Kathleen Corley's research indicates that in classical Greece, women were generally absent from meals, even within the household; but in Rome during the end of the Republic, women might be present at public meals in the household, if only for the first part of the meal (see Corley 2002). In more aristocratic Roman circles, women were occasionally included to render sexual favors to the male guests. In the inclusive Gospel meals, it appears that no distinction was made either in the name of gender, social class, or ethnic difference.

Quite likely such groups were not just once-off, chance events, but became more frequent and regular as participants gained courage, wisdom, and self-confidence. Incarnational, earthly transformation was happening long before the theological rhetoric that in time would begin to divide, exclude, and alienate people from the empowering praxis of Gospel commensality.

Jerome Neyrey (1996), in his reflections on the practice of commensality in Mark's Gospel, makes this astute observation: (1) bread is frequently mentioned (Mark 6:38–44, 52, 7:2–5, 27–28, 8:4–10, 16–21); and (2) while the Pharisees seem to be preoccupied with hands, lips, and bodily surfaces, Jesus seeks engagement with the heart and interior bodily states (Mark 7:1–23). Neyrey explains how Mark presents Jesus as challenging both the macrocosmic view of a world classified by purity and pollution (1996, 105–24) and the microcosmic replication of this in terms of how he ate, with whom he ate, and what he ate. In Mark 7, Jesus criticizes concern for bodily exterior (washing of hands and vessels, lip observance of God) and focuses on interior purity (an obedient heart, a virtuous soul). The view of the physical body attributed to Jesus, then, is less controlled than that credited to the Pharisees; and each view of the physical body is replicated in the relatively open or closed social relations that each practiced. Thus Jesus denounces the Judean social values of ethnic and religious separateness in favor of a more deeply embracing love and empowering inclusivity.

Both Jesus and Paul declare all foods to be clean (Mark 7:19; 1 Cor. 10:25–15; see Acts 10:15; see also more in Neyrey 1991). Food is God's primary nourishing gift from the sustaining earth itself. As indicated by Robert Karris (1985), food in Gospel lore is meant to be relished and cherished and used to forge circles of empowering inclusivity, not to become a divisive ideological basis for social division and religious rivalry.

Disciples of the Empowering Banquet

In the time of Jesus, the banquet normally referred to the symposium meal, with an aristocratic flavor, male dominated, and performed according to several elaborate rites and rituals. In time, the concept of the banquet did take on political and counter-cultural significance, paving the way for a more liberating critique of Roman imperialism. Meanwhile the Gospels bear evidence to another kind of banquet, usually described as friendship meals, rituals of solidarity for those belonging to what some commentators describe as "the little tradition" (Crossan 1991; Herzog 1994), the antidote to the domination of the great imperial practices. Gospel meals were not banquets in any comparable sense, other than in terms of what they achieved as empowering rituals, and in this regard they would have matched and even superseded the large-scale banquet.

In our endeavor to reclaim the inclusive empowerment of Gospel liberation—and honoring the subversive import of the Gospel meals—it seems absolutely right that we describe such experiences as banquets in their own right. It is the banquet invitation encapsulated in the words: "I have come that they may have life and have it to the full" (John 10:10). It is not a banquet awaiting us after a life of poverty and deprivation here on earth, but an incarnational feast of a God of unconditional love, seeking inclusive justice and empowering liberation for all. This provocatively original vision is best encapsulated in the power of poetry:

The Banquet as Subversive Metaphor

The banquet is a metaphor for the blessings all can share,
And the banqueting encounter requires special love and care.
It's the moment to leave everything behind,
The concerns round which we're oft preoccupied.
While we're called to make available to all
The devotion of our fellowship no shortcuts to install
The Banquet we must never compromise.

The banquet is a metaphor from which no one is excused
And the welcome to the banquet must never be refused.

"I've bought a field I need to cultivate;
A herd of healthy cattle to the market I must take;
I have married a wife, I need time to adjust,
An exclusive relationship demanding time and trust."
Excuses from the Banquet we often compromise.

The banquet is a metaphor subversively aligned
In favour of the "anawim," exploited and maligned.
To the highways and the bye-ways we must go,
The poor and maimed, and all condemned so low.
For the banquet hall is their's by very right
And tables are all set for their delight.
The Banquet we must never compromise.

The banquet is a metaphor for creation's plenitude,
Abundant are the gifts to receive in gratitude.
The daily bread to nourish us in strength,
Earth's fruitfulness becomes our daily drink.
And when there's food left over, we never hoard or waste
Like the Eucharistic table which welcomes every caste.
The Banquet we must never compromise.

Creation is a banquet hall we too often segregate,
With millions who are starving, despairing at the gate.
With economic crudity we viciously exploit,
Dividing up the planet, such violence we incite.
The highways and the bye-ways too long we have ignored,
While the rich have robbed the banquet hall where all the
        goods were stored,
Denying to all creation the abundance of the feast!

The Scandalous Exclusion

The womanist Afro-American theologian, Shawn Copeland, has
written extensively on the embodied experience of black women
who, for centuries, have borne in their bodies the identities and

pathologies that arise from oppression and exclusion. She high-lights the mental colonization that still infiltrates not only our politics and economics, but our religions and theology as well. Invoking patristic wisdom from St. Gregory of Nyssa (335–95), she addresses the exclusion from the Eucharistic table today with these piercing words:

> If my sister and brother is not at the table, we are not the flesh of Christ. If my sister's mark of sexuality must be obscured, if my brother's mark of race must be dis-guised, if my sister's mark of culture must be repressed, then we are not the flesh of Christ. It is through and in Christ's own flesh that the "other" is my sister, is my brother; indeed, the "other" is me . . . "The establish-ment of the Church is recreation of the world. But it is only in the union of all the particular members that the beauty of Christ's body is complete." [Gregory of Nyssa]. (Copeland 2010, 82)

It is sometimes described as the great scandal of contem-porary Christianity, particularly in the Catholic Church (to which Shawn Copeland belongs), which refuses participation in Eucharist to a range of people deemed not to be worthy of being included. If anything is crystal clear from the Gospels, it is the fact that those deemed to be most unworthy were precisely the ones who had the primary right to be at table with Jesus. No dis-tinction is made between the righteous and the sinner. Not only are all welcome, but all are fully embraced and included. There are no exceptions to the inclusivity of the open table.

Nor must we ever overlook the economic and political sig-nificance of Gospel commensality. The inclusive, open table is not only a challenge to a revolutionary new way of sharing the food on a social and religious basis. It is also an unambiguous declara-tion that the whole creation should be seen as an open table in which there is abundance for all to relish. This is currently not the case because the cruel economics and corrupt politics don't allow it to happen. This economic and political undercurrent is at the core of Gospel commensality and has been subverted for far too long. Hal Taussig (2009, 140) makes the bold claim that "from both the external and internal perspectives, it was the meal behavior that was at the heart of the emerging opposition between early Christians and Roman imperial power." Meals were a central feature of the various associations that empowered people in social cohesion and the ability to challenge oppressive and unjust forces.

Mark W. Stamm (2006), Professor of Christian Worship at Perkins School of Theology, provides an inspiring overview on how to revise our Eucharistic practice so that it reflects more proactively the open table of Gospel commensality. He challenges forthrightly the reluctance of his own Methodist Church (and others) who fail to make exception for those not officially baptized. His passion for a Eucharistic table open to all, irrespective of Christian background, is a growing aspiration of contemporary adult Christians, a quality of inclusivity, unambiguously mandated by the Gospels themselves.

Of all the examples of Gospel inclusivity explored in this book, the unconditional invitation to the open table may well be the most radical. Correspondingly, it is one of the most neglected and perverted of Gospel mandates. It is unlikely that mainline churches are going to embrace the inclusivity highlighted in the present chapter. It will be up to the adult people of God—in their homes and close affiliations—to adopt a new bold, subversive creativity and transcend the painful exclusions that have prevailed in the Christian churches for far too long.

Chapter 7

Subverting Greek Rationality

Dominant forms of reason—economic, political, scientific and ethical/prudential—are failing us because they are subject to a systematic pattern of distortions and illusions in which they are historically embedded and which they are unable to see or reflect upon.

— VAL PLUMWOOD

Why were the Gospels written in Greek? Chiefly because Greek was considered the appropriate language of the time for all serious engagement with culture, economic, politics, and religion. It was also deemed to be the most effective language for social communication. If you wanted to get your message circulating in circles where it might make a difference, use Greek. If you wanted your message taken seriously by the intellectuals of the time, use Greek. Greek was deemed to be the up-and-coming language for the advancement of human culture and for the reinforcement of human power.

The civilization of ancient Greece—the classical period—began around 700 BC and ended around 150 BC. Initially

101

society was divided into a militarized aristocracy and a larger group of free landowners. As the Greek economy became more commercialized, the society became more diverse and hierarchic. Frequent war produced a greater dependence on slavery and reduced emphasis on improved manufacturing technology. Greek society remained dominated by an aristocratic, land-owning elite. Greek politics and art was largely aristocratic in tone. Greek society depended on commerce but assigned relatively low social status to merchants. Like other ancient agricultural economies, the Greeks adopted slavery and were distinctively disempowering in their regard for women.

Greek culture and philosophy rested on four dominant characteristics:

1. Concern with personal salvation through mystical union with God;
2. Emphasis on tradition as a guide to action;
3. The use of reason as the means for discovering truth; and
4. Belief in the need for strong, authoritarian government.

Greek culture was predicated on the dominance of a literate, aristocratic elite, for which the values of the logical and the rational always held priority.

Leading names include those of Socrates, Plato, and Aristotle. The latter played a crucial role in the theology of St. Thomas Aquinas and the subsequent evolution of scholastic philosophy. For Aristotle, the perfect form of the human soul is *reason* separated from all connection with the body, hence fulfilling its activity without the help of any corporeal organ and so imperishable. By reason, the apprehensions, which are formed in the soul by external sense impressions and may be true or false, are converted into knowledge. *For reason alone can attain to truth either in cognition or action.* According to Aristotle, males can exercise the power of reason to the fullest; it is doubtful if women possess this endowment at all.

Exclusion: The Ideological Base

While Roman imperialism can be viewed as the basis for Christianity's addiction to imperial power, and the disempowering exclusions that arise thereafter, the adoption of Greek philosophy is an older and more subtle foundation for the dualistic split between those deemed worthy to be in, and those always kept on the outside. The Australian ecofeminist, Val Plumwood (2002, 4) provides a damning critique of what she describes as the irrationality of rationalist forms of reason. She further asserts: "Reason has been made a vehicle for damnation and death. . . . It is not reason itself that is the problem, I believe, but arrogant and insensitive forms of it that have evolved in the framework of rationalism and its dominant narrative of reason's mastery of the opposing sphere of nature and disengagement from nature's contamination elements of *emotion, attachment and embodiment*" (Plumwood 2002, 5; emphasis mine).

Whatever may have been the intention of Aristotle, and other Greek visionaries of classical period, subsequent generations, including Christians, adopted rational reason as the foundation stone for discerning and promoting truth. This ensued in a spirituality full of cerebral analysis, metaphysical theory, and epistemological distinctions. Not only did it create disconnection from the natural world, as Plumwood intimates, it also split the human soul from the body, spirit from matter, and the sacred from the mundane. And it left us with a serious incarnational impoverishment around emotion, attachment, and embodiment.

Prioritizing rational reason above all other forms of thought, perception, and discourse laid the foundations for what effectively became a powerful ideology, one that prevails almost unassailed to the present time. And it has exclusion deeply inscribed within it. Only those that can stand apart from their emotional attachments, from their deep embodied love for life—understood in human or ecological terms—may be deemed to be authentic human creatures. We are dealing with an anthropology seriously devoid of incarnational giftedness.

There is also a chronological reductionism that makes this ideology even more destructive. It works on the assumption that all humans who existed before the time span of our "civilized age," that is, living before 5000 BCE, should be regarded as essentially inhuman, perhaps, even nonhuman. They had not attained the sophisticated level to use the power of reason. So, where does that leave their ingenious ability to employ ritualized burials over one hundred thousand years ago, the evolution of language, and the skillful repertoire of Ice Age art? Those committed to the use of reason assume not only a total lack of reason in these prehistoric, complex developments, but more preposterously, a conviction that the rational God had nothing to do with such evolutionary breakthroughs. In other words, the cultural ideology has also become a religious one. Even God stands condemned as being irrational!

In a previous work, I try to deal with petrified reductionism to which all the formal religions have condemned our sacred human story of seven million years. It saddens me that so few theologians—none as far as I know—have attempted a redefinition of *incarnation* in the light of this now vastly expanded understanding of God's creativity at work in our human story. Presumably, the barrier once more is one of having to stick with rationality.

Jesus and the Cult of Rationality

Christian commentators often seem to miss a central nuance to the Gospel parables: they do not make rational sense! Nor, are they meant to. Preachers and teachers alike try to provide an explanation to make simple the complex message of many parables. This, I suggest, is a gross disservice—verging on blasphemy—to the subversive wisdom of parabolic lore.

When the Pharisees, and his own disciples, approach Jesus and ask for clarification on the meaning of the Kingdom of God, we need to note that Jesus does not offer a rationally coherent explanation. He responds with a parable: "The Kingdom of God may be compared to . . ." This is not the kind of response one would have expected in a culture devoted to maintaining rational truth. It is a dislocating gesture, suggesting that Jesus seeks to transcend the norms and expectations of rationality, inviting his hearers into a more expansive sphere of vision and possibility.

Several of the scenarios depicted in the parables are anything but rational. Many years ago, the Scripture scholar, C. H. Dodd (1978) identified the parabolic process as a three-way movement of orientation, disorientation, and reorientation. In the story of the Good Samaritan, a man is lying wounded and half-dead on the side of the road: the listener is oriented to the plight of the person but also to his possible ritually impure condition, confirmed by the priest and Levite walking on the other side of the road. The rational way of behaving defines the orientation.

Next comes the disorientation, which, in the historical context, would have been communicated primarily through the tone of the storyteller's voice in what was predominantly an oral culture. And the oral message was undoubtedly one inviting and challenging the hearers to forego the religious barriers with their accompanying prohibitions and do everything necessary to embrace and include the injured man. And then the disorientation goes wild—even crazy. The act of radical inclusivity is performed by a Samaritan, a despicably hated outsider for the Jewish people. This transgresses every known boundary, religious and cultural alike. This is not mere disorientation; it is major transgression.

Will a reorientation take place? Not likely! Instead the hearers are likely to turn on the storyteller and expel him from their midst! As the Gospels indicate elsewhere, this is intolerable language—precisely because it lacks rationality! The reorientation—the conversion toward radical inclusivity—is unlikely for the law-abiding, religiously faithful Jews. It may work for the Gentiles, and particularly those disenfranchised economically and socially, but one wonders how extensive will the impact be? This is an "irrational" paradigm shift with almost frightening implications. All the prohibitions, barriers, and exclusions have been dismantled. Nobody excluded anymore! Everybody, without a single exception, must be embraced and fully included.

The people most likely to get the message—and embrace the reorientation—are those who were robbed of their land, marginalized and deprived; they are the outsiders of a vicious system of exploitation and oppression. The parables offer no simple solution, but they sow seeds of conscientization, arousing people out of the complacency and passivity in which they can all too easily become enmeshed. The parable seeks to awaken the oppressed ones to challenge the oppressor, to speak truth to power, to find a language to denounce the oppressive rationality that seeks to justify—and even sanctify—the plight of those disempowered and excluded. It is in the parables more than anywhere else that we witness a Jesus who transcends the sinister trap of rational ideology—and always with a view to set free empowering inclusivity.

The People Hung on to His Words

They sought to destroy him, he threatened their power,
His words and his actions the people devour.
While the system resources deplete
and they struggle for daily needs meet,
they detect new empowerment released.
So they cling to his words as echoes endure
knowing deep in their hearts a hope that is true.

Words spoken wisely, subversively real,
The parable story no power can conceal.

The workers exploited too long,
a Samaritan can't get it wrong,
A woman with heaven's new song.
The tables are turned on the temple's regime
with chaos released for a dangerous dream.

His words are a treasure to hold in the heart,
empowering companions a breakthrough to start.
The freedom that all hearts desire
set free all the captives beyond the Empire
and liberate new life with hearts set on fire.
2000 years later, the people still cling
to empowering words and the hope that they bring.

What Do We Make of Centurion Inclusivity?

Rationality and the irrational come face to face in the intriguing story of the Roman centurion who comes to Jesus pleading for his sick servant (Matt. 8:5–13; Luke 7:1–10), described by Luke as a *doulos* (slave) and by Matthew as a *pais* (child). Firstly, we note the transgressive nature of the relationship between Jesus and the centurion. Obviously, the centurion knew enough about Jewish custom to understand that pious Jews did not enter Gentile homes. He was a Roman soldier, a man who shed blood for a living, and a leader of the occupying army, all of which should have kept Jesus far away from him and from his dwelling place as well. The centurion and the crowd were undoubtedly shocked that Jesus agreed to go to the officer's home.

One wonders if Luke is trying to circumvent the discomfort of the situation, informing us that the centurion had built the local synagogue and was said to love the Jewish people. Unlike the story found in Luke, Matthew indicated no preexisting relationship of the centurion with the Jewish community of Capernaum. And the centurion's own protest—that he was not worthy to have Jesus enter his home—could indicate the centurion's awareness of religious and cultural barriers.

Despite the various ambiguities that may have prevailed between a Jewish Jesus and a Gentile Roman military leader, the child is restored to health in what seems to be one of the few recorded instances of distant healing in the Gospels. Cultural and religious boundaries are once more transcended, despite some postcolonial objections to an underlying collusion (on the part of Jesus) with the forces of Roman oppression.

There is another dimension to this narrative wherein rationality and the irrational become intriguingly entwined. We recall that in the first-century AD Roman law prohibited heterosexual marriage for serving Roman soldiers. Among the Roman legions, this contributed to a homo-social environment in which males may have engaged in same-sex relationships (which should not be labeled as homosexual, as the term did not exist at the time).

In ancient Greece, the word *pais* was widely used and understood as referring to someone in a same-sex relationship. It was not unusual for Roman centurions and Roman soldiers to have male servants with whom they had a sexual liaison. When the centurion refers to "my *pais*" and then demonstrates extraordinary devotion to him—it is unlikely that a soldier would care so much about a mere slave—crossing every social boundary to beg for the help of an itinerant Jewish preacher. One needs to consider as sincerely as possible a psychosexual scenario that mainline scholarship would wish to bypass because of the complex moral implications.

Dr. Robert Gagnon (2001, 163, n.6), reputed to be an anti-gay scholar, concedes that in this story we are quite probably looking at a same-sex partnership. Other Christian scholars who support this interpretation include the Australian, Stuart Edser (2012), Theodore Jennings (2003) and Jack Clark Robinson (Jesus, the Centurion and his Lover, www.glreview.org/article/article-32/). One critical question arising from this reflection centers on the Greek rational culture of the time, indicating that the heterosexual couple relationship was the normative basis for a sexual relationship, with the primary purpose being the procreation of new life. In the engagement with the centurion, is Jesus also transcending that rationality, inviting the hearer to alternative ways of understanding human sexuality, the human desire for intimacy, and even the foundational purpose of human sexuality?

A complex "irrational" text like this should not simply be sanitized to sidestep complex psychosexual issues; nor should it be used merely to support contemporary debates related to homosexuality. My interest in the narrative is how best to investigate the lengths Jesus went to in order to embrace diversity and complexity, to include—and where possible never exclude—anyone, no matter how unconventional or transgressive their behavior might be.

An Irrational Answer?

According to Luke 7:19–20 (parallel of Matt. 11:2–3), John the Baptist, from his prison, sent two disciples to ask Jesus: "Are you the one who is to come, or should we expect someone else?" Knowing John to have been an ardently loyal follower of Jesus, and declaring his divine status at the baptismal scene, Christians have been understandably perplexed by John's apparent doubt and anxiety. Scholars have tried to resolve the dilemma by offering one or all of these explanations:

- Most of the early church leaders couldn't deal with the concept of a doubting John, so they argued that John is trying to reassure his disciples to hold on to their faith that Jesus was indeed the Messiah.
- Although the Gospels assure us that John knew Jesus' identity at the river Jordan, some wonder if this was more of an idyllic/mystical experience, whereas in fact, John's faith in Jesus is only progressively growing and developing.

- Still, others argue that being in prison could have depressed John and that he just needed reassurance. But John was a pretty strong character, so capitulating to depression seems unlikely.
- Some argue that John's question was one of "impatience" with Jesus because he was not delivering the liberation many expected of him.
- Others claim that John was "puzzled" because he had different expectations of the Messiah, perhaps similar to those expressed by the two disciples on the road to Emmaus. ("We expected him to be the one who would set Israel free.").
- Some even say that John was "disappointed" in Jesus because he wasn't doing what John expected him to do: overthrow Herod.

Did John like others at the time of Jesus expect the promised Messiah to be a political-type deliverer, and was John growing impatient because the breakthrough was not happening as fast as he had hoped? Jesus was spending time with the poor people, those who had been marginalized, those who were destitute. He was teaching them about God's love, proclaiming the imminent New Reign of God, while healing and restoring their broken lives. On the surface, he wasn't trying to claim political power. He wasn't confronting Herod. He certainly wasn't adopting or supporting a violent attack on the Romans.

And to John's disciples, Jesus gives this response: "Go and tell John what you have heard and seen. The blind are now able to see, and the lame can walk. People with leprosy are being healed, and the deaf can hear. The dead are raised to life, and the poor are hearing the good news. God will bless everyone who doesn't reject me because of what I do." (Matt. 11:4–6, CEV version). These words are generally interpreted as the Messianic promise outlined in Isaiah 35 and 42, indicating that Jesus indeed is the expected Messiah, thus reassuring John and his disciples in the face of their fears and doubts. We are not told how John felt about this response.

Taken at its face value, the text evokes this quality of rational response. But can we be sure that rationality is the appropriate vein in which to read either the question from John, or, more particularly, the response from Jesus? Among other things, we are dealing with a question of identity. Effectively, the disciples are asking, "Who exactly are you?" Throughout the Gospels, Jesus engages questions of identity with the rhetoric of parable rather than rational speech. Why not adopt the same strategy here?

A rational answer to the question would ensue in Jesus pointing the finger at himself and describing himself as the Messiah or adopting a set of characteristics to illuminate his God-given mission. As Robert Funk (1996) suggested many years ago, the direction of the pointing finger may be highly suggestive and rich in symbolic meaning. Jesus points the finger *away* from himself and not toward himself. And what does he point it toward?

"The blind see, the deaf hear." Is this not the New Reign of God taking shape? Is Jesus not pointing his finger directly at the Companionship of Empowerment? So, what is he actually saying to the disciples of John? "Stop looking at me the individual savior, and look instead toward my relational matrix, the web of my mission, from which I the individual—and you too—receives the divine mandate." Is Jesus confronting the disciples of John with a whole new sense of what it means to be a person: incarnational, inclusive, and empowering? Is he not challenging the disciples to cease gaping at some divine isolated hero and look instead at the empowering divine presence in their midst, embodied in the communal web of creation itself? Is this not what Scripture scholar, Marcus Borg has in mind in his frequent allusions to "the community that is Jesus?"

Are we not once more encountering parabolic speech, transcending the rationality that had become so normalized and expected in the dominant Greek culture? In fact, we may be engaging in hermeneutical depths that make more sense if we adopt the contemporary field of study known as queer theory (described in Chapter 11). In responding to the disciples of John, Jesus is not only confounding their rational uncertainties, but queering the very basis of human personhood itself.

According to Platonic and Aristotelian philosophy, authentic human personhood is defined by the ability to stand in autonomous self-reliance, over against, and superior to, all other forms of life, and clearly differentiated from the material creation itself. And the authentic human makes this option mainly through the use of reason (rationality). This is the understanding of the human person that dominated the early Christian centuries and today is extensively adopted throughout the civilized world. It is now so taken for granted that nobody ever dreams of questioning its hegemony.

It is a dysfunctional understanding of human personhood that is at the root of many of the major problems facing humanity today. It is not the human self-understanding that has sustained us for most of our long evolutionary journey on this earth; nor is it congruent with the mystical spirituality of times past or present. Today transpersonal psychology is reconnecting with, and seeking to reclaim, the deeper more ancient sense of human selfhood, often encapsulated in the statement "I am at all times the sum of my relationships and that is what defines my identity." Is this what the historical Jesus was declaring in pointing the finger away from his individual self toward the relational context that determined and defined his individual identity in the first place? Was Jesus using the moment to deliver not a rational answer but an archetypal response with implications stretching far beyond the immediacy of the query brought by John's disciples?

Inclusive Personhood

Jesus did not give the disciples of John a rational answer. In fact, Jesus rarely gives a rational response to any query or question.

Whether or not this indicates that Jesus is deliberately confronting the invasive Greek culture of the time is something we will never be able to verify. What we cannot evade is the invitation to queering the prevailing mode of personhood, stretching it beyond the robust individualism that would nurture imperial power, toward an inclusivity programmed for mutual empowerment.

While Plato and Aristotle are often credited with a wisdom that evolved into more civilized ways of being in the world, that understanding of civilization is heavily influenced by the culture of patriarchy. We note this in Aristotle's dismissal of women as essentially nonrational beings, whose primary function is to serve as biological organisms providing the forum for fertilizing the male seed. Greek anthropology of the classical period is heavily rooted in biology, male biased, dualistic, and primed for winners to the exclusion of losers. It is highly unlikely that Jesus adopted this anthropology—for himself or for anybody else.

This leaves us with a theological quandary of serious import: what anthropology underpins our understanding of the Christian notion of Incarnation? The Councils of Nicea and Chalcedon responded in terms of the classical Greek understanding of the human person. And it appears that most theologians—and the teaching authority of the church—have never dreamed of questioning the underlying assumptions.

Multiple Belonging

Jesus' response to the disciples of John embodies a very different way of being human—in our relation to God, to humanity, and to the world. It is a relational paradigm, characterized by inclusivity and mutual empowerment. It seeks to break down all imperial bastions of power, and break through all the barriers that exclude and segregate. It seeks a new world order, devoid of the social stratification of shame and honor, embracing unambiguously a conviviality where we call each other servants no longer but call forth one and all in a new circle of empowering friendship (cf. John 15:15).

More controversially, the Australian theologian, Gideon Goosen (2011, 53–74), discerns this new human relationality as foundational to the *religious multiple belonging* that characterizes our time and pushes religious inclusivity toward a quality of integration largely unknown among the monotheistic religions. The fear of religious relativism, preoccupying formal religionists in our time, might well be another defense against the threat of the "irrational." Monotheism, as indicated later, is not just about singular devotion to the God who is one. It is a patriarchal, imperial declaration that my God is superior to all others, excludes all others, and subconsciously seeks to eliminate all others.

The prevailing rationality is that of the patriarchal philosophy of divide and conquer. Today, overtly and subconsciously millions are turning their backs on this violent exclusionary ideology, seeking engagement and whole new partnerships with diverse cultures and religions.

Instead of viewing multiple religious belonging as a postmodern fickleness, it marks, in many cases, a new spiritual threshold embraced by adults seeking to cocreate a world of peace, justice, and articulations of solidarity that transcend the inherited rational distinctions of nation, tribe, and religious conformity.

Rationality, as traditionally defined, is a smokescreen for several forms of patriarchal oppression, which often translate into dualistic splitting between the favored insiders and the many that must be kept outside. The inherited culture insists that the suppression of rationality automatically means an irrational reign of terror. This is another dualistic split that cannot tolerate or employ the fertile middle ground of parabolic wisdom. The new future of the Christian Gospel, and the future that brings promise and hope to humanity today, is one of radical inclusivity, seeking to outgrow the many divisions and distinctions inherited from an overly rationalistic past. A daunting challenge—and one that Christians should embrace with inspiring audacity!

Chapter 8

Let's Bring in the Stigmatized Subalterns

An Aristotelian hierarchy of the sense is largely presumed as normative.

— Louise J. Lawrence

The culture of a people is an ensemble of texts ... which the anthropologist strains to read over the shoulders of those to whom they properly belong.

— Clifford Geertz

I borrow the concept of the *subaltern* from the field of postcolonial studies. Its origins are often traced to the Italian Marxist thinker, Antonio Gramsci, primarily concerned about those individuals and groups deprived of social and political agency because of their exclusion from society's democratic processes. In contemporary postcolonial research, its best-known advocate is the Indian scholar Gayatri Chakravorty Spivak, for many years professor of literature at Columbia University (United States). She is best known for the essay "Can the Subaltern Speak," referring to

115

marginalized groups and lower classes who have been rendered without *agency* because of their social status.

Spivak distinguishes between the oppressed and those of subaltern status. In several contemporary cultures, minority groups may be oppressed but can still exercise a voice, socially, politically, and economically. The subaltern is without representative voice, as one notes among many refugees and asylum seekers in the contemporary world. There are several other connotations to the word, denoting an oppressive invisibility because of ethnicity, gender, disability, and the various kinds of marginality accompanying perceptions and projections of being other than what the dominant culture deems to be acceptable and normative.

Thus in mainstream Christianity, strong concern for the poor and marginalized is expressed even in official church teachings. However, *poor* and *marginalized* can be very slippery terms, often used in colonial rhetoric with dangerously ambivalent meanings. By expressing concern for the underclasses, the imperial system can project a benign exterior whereas inner motivation may be manipulative and oppressive. Occasionally the churches collude with imperial domination to name and highlight significant others on whom it can project its negative and derogatory perceptions, and on whom it can displace blame to exonerate its own performance. Here we encounter a range of subtle projections often leading to those forms of exclusion and debilitation envisaged in the disempowering plight of the subaltern.

The Disabled Subaltern

In this chapter, I want to examine the plight of those Gospel personalities exhibiting various forms of disability, which in the culture of the time often rendered them unworthy (translate: incapable) of exercising a social, political, or economic voice. Such is the cultural plight of those described as blind, deaf, maimed, or possessed by evil spirits: they are effectively condemned to a subaltern status. In particular, how do we revision an inclusively empowering role for those religiously condemned because of evil spirit possession? Have we overspiritualized and exorcised these subalterns to a point where we may be missing clues inviting other kinds of cultural and spiritual discernment.

We review the plight of those categorized as disabled: the blind, the deaf, those unable to speak (mute), the lame (paralyzed). Not only are such people socially and politically disempowered, but they tend to be exploited for a whole range of reasons serving the maintenance and advancement of imperial power. In the reflections that follow, I am particularly indebted to the British Scripture scholar, Louise Lawrence, for her incisive analysis of Gospel disability outlined in her book, *Sense and Stigma in the Gospels* (2013).

Building on the work of Jewish scholar, Yael Avrahami, on sensory anthropology, Lawrence notes that throughout the Bible sensory disabilities are often associated with divine punishment and rejection of opponents: "Divine chastisement for example was often meted out through the senses (Deut. 28:28–29) and warriors too sought to inflict physical damage on sense organs to indicate the loser's surrender and inferiority . . . the sensory disabled are in effect rendered as non-persons" (Lawrence 2013, 15). Quoting from Saul Olyan's *Disability in the Hebrew Bible* (2008), Lawrence suggests that disability in the Scriptures is often associated with weakness, vulnerability, dependence, and ineffectuality, creating structures of exclusion and disempowerment that are rarely named or confronted in biblical lore. According to Wendy Cotter (2010, 42) Bartimaeus is the only healed person in the Gospels who is actually identified by name.

In the Gospels, disability is often attributed to human sin, one's own or that of one's ancestors. More frequently, it is assumed to be the result of possession by evil spirits. Much more serious is the tendency to attribute disability to an incapacity or unwillingness to behave religiously. Blindness is often equated with being spiritually in the dark; deafness is associated with an inability to hear God speak, and being unable to speak renders one defective in being able to give glory to God. Both the leper and blind man rely on others to activate a resolution to their plight, identifying disability with disempowering codependency.

Perhaps the most awkward question of all arising from such considerations is the ambiguous and collusive role adopted by—or attributed to—Jesus when dealing with human disability. We never hear of Jesus embracing blind, deaf, or mute persons simply for who they are as human beings living with human limits, and perhaps doing so with admirable resilience often within a culture where the shame-honor dynamic caused serious social dislocation for such persons. Instead of admiring and reinforcing their resilience, Jesus is consistently portrayed as rectifying and eliminating disabilities in order to raise such people to the standards of the dominant culture. Nor does Jesus ever invite such healed people to become disciples.[1]

Lawrence (2013, 41–44) cites the example of blind Scripture scholar, John Hull, who clearly feels excluded and oppressed by the Gospel emphasis on blindness as a metaphor for a lack of spiritual understanding. Hull is understandably critical of the fact that Jesus' ministry as imaged in the Gospels was focused on restoration of sight rather than affirmation, compassion, and friendship to the blind. Jesus, as the evangelists construct him, operates by sight-centric values and thus conceives of the blind as an alien out-group. As Hull poignantly states, "You have led me by the hand out of blindness but you would not have been my companion during my blindness" (Lawrence 2013, 43).

Throughout the Gospels, sighted people take priority for being enlightened and capable of understanding at levels superior to those lacking sight. Is this a religious/cultural prejudice whereby blindness is regarded as some kind of curse, or worse, a form of demon possession? In the case of Bartimaeus, a congenitally blind man, we hear the disciples ask "Rabbi, who sinned, this man or his parents that he was born blind?" Insofar as such prejudices seem to be endorsed in Gospel encounters, with the accompanying systemic and social exclusion, we need to ask "Is this the choice of the evangelist, a later interpreter, or Jesus himself?" Rarely, if ever, does Jesus confront such prejudices.

In dealing with those afflicted with deafness and the inability to speak (mute), the disability is frequently attributed to the influence of evil spirits. Obviously this attribution needs to be understood in its cultural context where many forms of illness were understood to be caused by malignant spiritual forces. We need to remember that such ancient cultures were also richly endowed with ritual resources and skills to alleviate such afflictions. For instance, using saliva and spitting were behaviors adopted by many exorcists (read: healers) in addressing human disability. Once again, my concern in raising such issues is the apparent lack of any redress by Jesus to dislodge the ensuing sense of disempowerment and social exclusion.

Jesus and Demon Possession

According to Matthew's Gospel (Matt. 8:16), "many who were demon-possessed were brought to him, and he drove out the spirits with a word and healed all the sick." The Greek term *evil spirit* appears twenty-one times in the New Testament. In the Gospel stories of demonic possession, temptation and sin is not the primary role played by demons, but rather the causing of disease, disability, mental illness, and antisocial behavior; the spirits defile and compel their human hosts to suffer both physically and spiritually. Although healing and exorcism are distinguished, they often appear in close association, and some afflictions are caused by demonic possession: the inability to speak (Matt. 9:32), blindness (Matt. 12:22), deafness (Mark 9:17–29, epilepsy (Matt. 17:18), and fever and other diseases (Luke 4:39, 8:2). Mental illness, however, was the most common result.

In her analysis of stigma and disability in the Gospels Louise Lawrence (2013, 98ff.) devotes a whole chapter to the case of the demon-possessed epileptic boy (Mark 9:17–29) in which she notes that in such episodes, it is the condition rather than the person with the condition who tends to be the focus of attention. And she concludes, "Bypassing the characters themselves, they are swamped by negative associations; at best they are helpless, hopeless and passive, and at worst degenerate, disordered and demonized. Once more the stories or potential agency of the individuals involved are eclipsed."

Beyond the plight of individuals, however, I'd like to raise the more complex question as to why the significance of spirit-power is so negatively portrayed in the Gospels, and if Jesus himself has been co-opted into the stigmatized portrayal of those deemed to be so depraved? And insofar as such demonization reinforces a culture of exclusion and disempowerment, does Jesus himself stand accused of oppressive collusion? These are complex questions far beyond my competence, but they do seem to be of central importance in an analysis of Gospel inclusivity. I raise them in the hope that others more enlightened than I can shed further light on such complex dynamics.

In several human cultures, ancient and modern, spirit-power tends to be portrayed negatively, despite the fact that indigenous people, ancient and modern, embrace a dynamic and empowering sense of belief in the Great Spirit. Such ancient faith has been the basis of an enduring relational spirituality bestowing sacredness on all created reality, combined with the ability to ritualize the invoking of spirit-power when confronted by calamity and suffering. Shamanism is one ancient practice in which possession by a *pneuma* could be a desired state of visionary trance, an endowment not for the devotee's self-aggrandizement, but to facilitate healing and wholeness for the surrounding community. Andrei Znamenski, associate professor of history at the University of Alabama, provides what in my opinion is one of the most comprehensive and informed accounts of Shamanism and its relation to ancient Christianity (Znamenski 2007).

Marcus Borg (1994a, 35–36), provides a useful overview of the cultural significance of Shamanism when he writes,

> Spirit persons are known cross-culturally. They are people who have vivid and frequent subjective experiences of another level or dimension of reality. These experiences involve momentary entry into non-ordinary states of consciousness and take a number of different forms. Sometimes there is a vivid sense of momentarily seeing into another layer of reality; these are visionary experiences. Sometimes there is the experience of journeying into that other dimension of reality; this is the classic experience of the shaman. Sometimes there is a strong sense of another reality coming upon one, as in the ancient expression "the Spirit fell upon me." Sometimes the experience is of nature or an object within nature momentarily transfigured by "the sacred" shining through it. . . . What all persons who have these experiences share is a strong sense of there being more to reality than the tangible world of our ordinary experience. They share a compelling sense of having experienced something "real." They feel strongly that they know something they didn't know before. Their experiences are noetic, involving not simply a feeling of ecstasy, but a knowing. What such persons know is the sacred. spirit persons are people who experience the sacred frequently and vividly. They mediate the spirit in various ways. Sometimes they speak the word or the will of God. Sometimes they mediate the power of God in the form of healings and/or exorcisms. Sometimes they function as game finders or rainmakers in hunting-and-gathering and early agricultural societies. Sometimes they become charismatic warriors and military leaders. What they all have in common is that they become funnels or conduits for

the power or wisdom of God to enter into this world. Anthropologically speaking, they are delegates of the tribe to another layer of reality, mediators who connect their communities to the Spirit.

Adopting such insights, the African Scripture scholar, Pieter Craffert (2008) explores a range of parallels between the healing work of Jesus and that of a conventional Shaman/ness, reinforcing several insights already surfaced by the Siberian Shamanic scholar, Gavriil Ksenofontov in the early twentieth century. In conclusion, Craffert (2008, 421) writes, "Like all shamanic figures, Jesus was credited with numerous healings, exorcisms, and various forms of spirit control. It is typical of shamanic figures to control spirit entities in the cultural settings in which they operate, and the bulk of the evidence regarding Jesus's public life could be interpreted in such a way as to show his control of spirits."

Craffert adopts language extensively used in the contemporary scholarly world, emphasizing the *control* of the spirit domain by shamans then and now. Controlling the spirit-force is usually understood as subjecting, disempowering, dislodging, disabling, and even getting rid of them. But is *control* the appropriate word? I suggest *appeasing* or *placating* may be more generic terms, particularly if evil spirits represent personal, interpersonal, or cultural articulations of *unmet needs*. People in the time of Jesus were victims of internalized oppression, coming from both outside (Roman) and within (Jewish religiosity). Not only were people struggling to survive, but, in the process of doing so, often repressed pain and trauma to levels that resulted in destructive behaviors often associated with demon possession. In which case the desperate plea may indicate the need to embrace and include a complex deeper truth, rather than expel and thus exclude what we perhaps too hastily judge to be a dangerous evil force.

Rita N. Brock, herself acquainted with the experience of personal trauma, comments on evil-possession in Mark's Gospel:

"Possession is not the result of personal sin and cannot be healed by private penance. The possession comes from relationships lived under the deceptions of unilateral power" (Brock 1992, 79). Anna Runesson (2011, 211) adds the following astute observation:

> Not only do Jesus's exorcisms deal directly with the subject of colonial oppression; they address the problem more to the point than would a straightforward confrontation between the Messiah and the Roman generals. Far from treating the symptom without addressing the disease, Jesus' exorcisms cut directly to the heart of the matter, even if a single exorcism leaves much more work to be done.

In other words, engagement with the spirit-world in the time of Jesus was considerably more complex than current moralistic criteria are capable of understanding. By the time of the historical Jesus, several cultures already knew and employed a type of mystical wisdom to engage what today we call the spirit world. This is an ancient cultural force that has been extensively undermined, to the point of being demonized by the emergence of the overrational metaphysical wisdom that characterized the Gospel writers Not only are people of that time being disempowered in terms of the social and cultural sense of agency (as Louise Lawrence suggests), they were further disenfranchised, but what was probably a predominantly empowering force is also extensively maligned, and the negative repercussions impact upon first nations (tribal) peoples in our own time.

Where Jesus stood on this critical issue is something we probably can never clarify, but it seems religiously irresponsible to go on assuming that Jesus fully supported and endorsed the demonization of spirit-power. That is probably a culturally defined perception imposed upon Jesus rather than one he himself would have totally embraced. In the Gospels we are introduced to merely one side of the spirit-imbued universe: the negative, destructive side; and in a classical Greek dualism, we are never allowed to consider other meanings belonging to the other half of the permutation.

Disability and Ritual Purity

Johnathan Klawans (2005) and a number of other scholars (mainly of Jewish persuasion), claim that most analysts exaggerate the significance of ritual purity in the time of Jesus, claiming that it was a requirement first and foremost for temple priests and only applied outside that context in a limited way. I follow the broader scholarly consensus that regards ritual purity as still a substantial social and religious issue at the time, one that forms the basis of several miracle stories. It seems to have been after the fall of Jerusalem in 70 CE that such ritual practices lost much significance for the newly Christian community.

According to Jerome H. Neyrey (1998) the social structure of Jewish society at the time of Jesus was characterized by a strong sense of internal lines and boundaries, illustrated in what he calls a map of persons. (Of course, Gentiles are not on the map of God's covenant people, nor are Samaritans).[2] In general, there were three areas where ritual purity was to be observed: purifying the body and hands, purifying vessels used for food preparation and serving, and eating only pure animals. And impurity could be contracted through association with any of the following: a corpse, a leper, a victim of a deadly illness, the carcass of an animal, menstruation and childbirth, sexual relations, eating unclean animals, and using ritually impure vessels.

Jesus tends to be portrayed as confronting forthrightly the exclusionary oppression related to ritual impurity (for an alternative view, see Meier 2009, 413–15). Such a prophetic liberating stance is not as obvious in his encounters with people with disabilities. On the surface, he seems to collude with many of the prevailing cultural exclusionary norms of the day, unless, of course, we shift the hermeneutical focus and view such disabilities from other nonmedical perspectives. We return briefly to the postcolonial optic.

In her analysis of the Gospel miracles, Wendy Cotter (2010, 212 n.40, 216–19, 224–31, 244–46), frequently alludes to a possible imperial undergirding for several of the miracle stories, more particularly in relation to possession by evil spirits. To what extent might many of these afflictions be metaphors for crippling conditions arising from internalized oppression caused by external Roman exploitation or internal disempowering religiosity? The story of the Garasene demoniac is an oft-cited example, with the many military allusions in the Greek text. Perhaps, this was not a case of a man being possessed by an evil spirit in the literal sense, but rather somebody driven insane because of the cruel suffering ensued from Roman occupation. Had his land been robbed? Had he been made homeless? Rejected by his family and loved ones? Or worse still, perhaps witnessed loved ones slaughtered before his eyes? John Dominic Crossan (1991) offers the intriguing interpretation of the pigs running into the sea as the symbolic routing of the Romans from the land of Israel, having observed that the boar (pig) was an insignia on some of the Roman military banners of the time.

How many of the disability stories in the Gospels might better be regarded as parables-in-action, confronting and addressing the disabling effects of internalized oppression, ensuing from external and internal oppressive forces? I address this issue at greater length in a previous work (O'Murchu 2011, 79ff.) and will not repeat the argument here. Jesus is not so much being dismissive of a person's genuine reality (as Lawrence intimates), but rather is evoking cultural healing and restoration of equilibrium to the disruption caused by the interfering forces of oppression. Important though this insight is, it still leaves us uneasy with the apparent cultural tendency to use human disability to promote other needs, leaving people like John Hull rightly feeling excluded and disempowered.

Finally, we also need to acknowledge the all too human Jesus who made some serious blunders at times. As indicated in a previous work (O'Murchu, 2011, 160ff.), I do not see this as a limitation in terms of Christian faith but as a significantly important theological insight. Christians claim that Jesus was fully divine but also fully human, and they mistakenly go on to suggest that because he was divine, he could make no human errors. *A person cannot be fully human without making mistakes.* A person incapable of making mistakes is not human in any meaningful sense of the word. Jesus made mistakes—in fact, I suspect he made many human blunders—and that is what makes him uniquely incarnational for Christian believers.

In his apparent disregard for people with human disabilities, did Jesus end up colluding with a culture that could not tolerate or accept what Louise Lawrence calls humans-with-limits? Quite possibly, yes! And to that extent, Jesus made some serious misjudgments that may well have left such vulnerable people feeling hurt and alienated. However, as indicated above, I suspect there is more to the healing miracle stories than what seems immediately obvious. These narratives are complex parablelike enterprises. *Internalized oppression* is probably the central issue, and the ensuing remedial action is not just about the immediate characters with disability but about a larger cultural liberation from the systemic forces that disable not only individual persons, but indeed entire nations, cultures, and peoples.

Gospel Inclusivity Today

All of this requires us to leave to one side the incomplete analysis of our ancient inherited wisdom. These are important historical, social, and theological explorations that will continue to engage specialists—long into the open-ended future. Important though such specialization is to the understanding and living of our Christian faith, its enduring truth and credibility belongs to those of us called to live it out each day in a way that enhances empowering inclusivity. We can easily get distracted by what exactly the historical Jesus did or did not do. Ultimately, the credibility and flourishing of Christian faith rests with what *we do* rather than analyzing in detail what Jesus may, or may not, have done.

An empowering transformative faith for the twenty-first century requires all of us to commit ourselves unambiguously and unrelentingly to the *Companionship of Empowerment*. Many Christian churches, preoccupied with pure doctrine and an often literal interpretation of Scripture, fail to embrace this ideal. People of disability, on the one hand, and millions socially and culturally disempowered, do not experience in a transparent way the empowering inclusivity of the Gospel. It is that disconnect of the twenty-first century, and not the incomplete picture of the first century, that should engage Christians now and for the future.

Scripture scholar, Walter Brueggemann has wrestled with the hermeneutical challenge of how to deconstruct the imperial ideology that has been so deeply insinuated in Christian sacred text and reclaim for the future a more empowering and liberating message:

> Interpretation is not the reiteration of the text. It is rather the movement of the text beyond itself in fresh ways, often ways never offered until this moment of utterance. . . . The power to articulate newness shatters all our cherished presuppositions and in turn pushes the question of authority outside the realm of explanation, leading into the world of testimony. . . . In the end, scripture is not a contest to see who can prevail in interpretation. It is rather an address that offers a "newness" and a "strangeness" that are out beyond all our pet projects. (Brueggemann 2005, xvii, 8, 28)

The present work is a nonscholarly attempt to captivate something of the newness and strangeness subverted in the radical inclusivity of Gospel wisdom and translate it afresh for "this moment of utterance" in which all Christians are asked to give witness (what Brueggemann calls *testimony*) to offer fresh inspiration and hope for the twenty-first century. We daily encounter a world fragmented and divided by adversarial conflict, often fueled by religious bigotry. If Christianity cannot bring reconciliation and healing to such a world, then it ends up as another irrelevant force or worse still another religious instrument creating division instead of wholeness and peace.

Basically, the thesis of this book is that Christianity has not taken seriously its foundational blueprint for wholeness, its archetypal sense of oneness that must never exclude or oppress anybody. Scholars may quibble about the interpretative evidence upon which I make this claim. It strikes me that the underlying evidence is sufficiently coherent, and today is indisputably needed, to bring about the new heaven and the new earth desired not only by Christian belief, but by people of good will in all the great religions of our age.

Chapter 9

The Cross:
An Option for Inclusive Solidarity

It is not Jesus' suffering and death that are redemptive, but his life as a praxis of protest—against injustice, and solidarity in defence of life. Suffering is a factor in the liberation process, not as a means of redemption, but as the risk that one takes when one struggles to overcome unjust systems whose beneficiaries resist change. The means of redemption is conversion, opening up to one another, changing systems of distorted relations, creating loving and life-giving communities of people here and now, not getting oneself tortured to death.

— ROSEMARY RADFORD RUETHER

Jesus' entire approach to changing society—changing the world—was based on the idea of non-violent resistance.

— NICK PAGE

Christianity has a long allegiance to the power of the Cross. Salvation in the power of the Cross frequently occurs in the Pauline letters. An elaborate Passion Narrative features in all four Gospels. The cult of Christian martyrdom draws its inspiration and impetus from what Jesus endured on the Cross. Not surprising, therefore, for much of Christian history, suffering in solidarity with Jesus has been exonerated as a more authentic way to holiness in this life and to eternal salvation in the life to come.

Devotion to the Cross of Jesus has served two main purposes. First, at a practical/pastoral level, it has proved to be an enormous source of comfort, strength, and reassurance for suffering people, whether because of personal circumstances (sickness, pain, personal tragedy) or extraneous forces arising from oppression, poverty, and social disempowerment. Second, the Cross is extensively viewed as the icon of salvation and redemption. It is in the power of Jesus' sacrifice on the Cross that our sins are wiped out and the curse of death is transformed for all time. Fidelity to the Cross—and the suffering that often accompanies it—is the royal road to happiness in a life hereafter. This latter, I will shortly describe as the "devotion of consolation."

Devotion to the Cross has kept millions closely affiliated with the Christian faith but in a capacity not conducive to empowering inclusivity. To the contrary, the penitential emphasis on suffering and self-abasement has been a very effective tool to keep people obedient and subservient. In this way the powerful exclusive domination of the patriarchal ecclesiastical system has remained intact for far too long.

Calvary's Disintegration

It is often suggested that after the untimely death of Jesus, his immediate followers were scattered, and were it not for the miracle of Pentecost (Acts 2), which helped to reassemble the fragmented male apostles, the Christian dream might well have come to naught. This account is a popularized patriarchal version of events based on several flawed assumptions. It does appear that the group known as *the twelve* were badly disenfranchised after the death of Jesus, disillusioned mainly by the fact that they expected Jesus to be some kind of political liberator (from Roman oppression), and when he failed to achieve that outcome, they capitulated to despair and disintegration.

Judging the major outcome in terms of the twelve—the in-group—is a patriarchal ploy determined to hold on to a predominantly male-led movement, postulated on a divine male Messiah, assumed to be an authentic representative of the great King David. It tends to ignore the complex nature of discipleship—*there were many other groups beside the twelve.* Of particular interest, from the perspective of Gospel inclusivity, is the group described as "the crowd"—outsiders, who tend to be portrayed as traitors. In truth, they followed Jesus with an enduring sense of fidelity—and did *not* betray him in the end as is popularly believed.

There are two groups of outsiders related to the death of Jesus—and to the cult of the Cross—that history has largely ignored, and Scripture scholarship has failed to discern: *the crowd and the women disciples.*

1. *The Crowd.* These seem to be the same people that followed him for much of his public ministry, and probably included many who were healed, welcomed to the open table, and empowered through the subversive words and deeds of Jesus. It is widely assumed that they betrayed him in the end and worse still called for his crucifixion (Mark 15:11–13). While Mark highlights their role with five distinct references, both Matthew and Luke reduce the allusions to three; John only retains a single reference (John 12:12–18). Borg and Crossan (2006)—pretty much single-handedly—challenged this popular view, suggesting that the negative portrayal of the crowd is a politically motivated distortion of the facts in order (a) to deflect attention from the Romans (and their collusion with Jewish authorities) and (b) to validate the punitive actions of the authorities

insinuating that even the people themselves wanted to get rid of this dangerous rebel.

Borg and Crossan (2006, 88–90, 144) highlight the fact that throughout the Holy Week narrative of Mark's Gospel the crowd consistently adopts a protective role: Sunday (Mark 11:8), Monday (Mark 11:18), and Tuesday (Mark 11:32, 12:12, 37). They distinguish between the faithful crowd and a much smaller group (located in Herod's palace) stirred up by the authorities to seek Jesus' execution. Jesus was arrested in the darkness apart from his large protective crowd and was crucified as swiftly as possible. Historians generally agree that the story of Pilate offering the crowd a choice of releasing Barabbas or Jesus (see Mark 15:6–15), with the crowd seeking the freedom of Barabbas, is generally considered to be fictitious. There is no non-Christian reference to the bizarre practice of giving complete amnesty to a prisoner—*any* prisoner chosen by a crowd—on festival days.

If the situation was as politically and religiously tense—as we are commonly led to believe—one could concede a degree of ambivalence among the crowd—lest they themselves end up being crucified. In justice, however, we must not negatively dismiss a group comprising the beneficiaries of Gospel empowerment. At one time very much outsiders, they are now the radical insiders, and their fidelity was probably more enduring than acknowledged in popular Christian lore.[1]

2. *The Women.* Although concrete evidence for the fidelity of the crowd is difficult to obtain (or has been substantially subverted), not so for the role played by the other outstanding outsiders, namely, Mary Magdalene and her companions (probably consisting of both males and females). Their presence is recorded in all four Gospels—faithful to the bitter end. The male apostles had fled, confused, and disillusioned. The women remained and saw through the brutal painful ordeal. And when it comes to Eas-

ter morning, it is the women who come to the fore, with Mary Magdalene herself receiving the commission to go and announce the news to the brethren. The Christian churches have not come to terms with this first strand of Christian discipleship—in most cases, they have not even begun to acknowledge it. We pick up the painful exclusion in the next chapter.

Jesus was crucified because of how he empowered rank-and-file people of the day. These are the people who constitute the crowd described in the Passion Narratives, and the women who remained faithful against great odds. The authorities were petrified, anticipating that the empowerment could cause serious political unrest, and a distinctive chance of a serious challenge to Roman imperialism in the land of Israel.

Once the Cross became synonymous with a devotion of submission, Christianity lost sight of the subversive political undercurrents. Death on a Cross (crucifixion) was primarily a punishment for subversives, for those who posed a threat to Roman imperialism or those who contravened patriarchal expectation, such as slaves protesting against their subservience. It was a cruel, barbaric death made as gruesome as possible to deter others from entertaining subversive action.

Consequently, for St. Paul, Jesus did not die—*he was killed.* Jesus was executed by imperial authority because of the threat he posed to their powerful hegemony. His commitment to the Companionship of Empowerment began empowering the masses (the outsiders) to a degree that the political and religious systems could no longer tolerate. Outsiders were growing in confidence, defying exclusion practices, rallying in solidarity (the crowds!), reclaiming their voice for justice (the women). Outsiders appropriating such emasculation could not easily be controlled. By eliminating the leader, the primary catalyst, the Romans (in collusion with the Jews) had hoped to undermine this new messianic uprising. They could not have been more mistaken.

The Devotion of Consolation

The Cross embraces outsiders in what initially will look like two diametrically opposed ways: (1) through *the devotion of consolation* and (2) by adopting *the spirituality of liberation.* The latter is the more authentic Christian option, promising long-term hope to the outsider. The former (the devotion of consolation) has had a long, historical appeal for outsiders (Christians and others), often depicted in the distraught, broken person crying out in desperation for God's mercy and forgiveness. It is a religious strategy adopted by millions of contemporary Christians, particularly the poor and disenfranchised. Rarely the subject of scholarly research, *the devotion of consolation* merits serious and informed discernment, precisely because of its extensive appeal.

The devotion of consolation includes practices such as

1. Beseeching God in prolonged prayer, often repeating set formulas, such as in the Catholic Rosary or adopting popular novenas;
2. Devoted attention to sacred objects such as medals, statues, relics;
3. Penitential acts such as fasting, flagellation;
4. Processions to honor a particular saint or holy person;
5. Pilgrimages to places of special devotion (e.g., Lourdes, Mecca, Armistar); and
6. Charitable deeds that obtain merit in a life hereafter (e.g., giving food to monks).

Typically, the devotee carries a deep desire to placate a distant, demanding God; the more devotions can be multiplied, the better the chances of the prayer (or petition) being answered. And even if it is not answered, it is hoped that the devotion and penance will mitigate the harsh judgment of God, and provide reassurance for the journey through this vale of tears to the joy and happiness of a life hereafter.

Three features of such popular devotion deserve considerable discernment.

1. Religion of every persuasion awakens inner sentiment, making the devotee receptive to transcendent meaning. Spirit encounters Spirit, evoking both emotional response and imaginative engagement. There follows a kind of psychic release, what mystics often describe as divine abandonment. It can be a warm reassuring feeling, leaving one in deep anguish and psychological trauma when such an experience is no longer available. The mystics describe such conditions as the dark night of the senses and, at a deeper level, the dark night of the soul.

2. There is a social dimension, resulting in people coming together whether for prayer, worship, or other devotional practices. It is impossible to differentiate the spiritual and psychological dimensions at work here. Spirit-power can operate through feelings, emotions, and even through physical gestures as the collective body dances, sings, acclaims, or swoons in ecstasy. In terms of Christian discernment, we need to establish if such people are empowered to live more holistically and become more proactive in bringing to the wider world greater purpose, dignity, and freedom. If the collective euphoria leads people to seek greater self-gratification, or a desire to reserve the wisdom and joy merely to their own ranks, then self-delusion and false hope may be at work. Neither the insider nor the outsider is being authentically empowered.

3. We need to attend to the human capacity and desire for ritual making. There are several overlaps here with the social dimension described above. Humans have been engaged in ritual making for at least seventy thousand years, long before religion or formal worship was ever envisioned. Ritual is an inner endowment, a facility for spiritual empowerment, shared by all humans, expressed

in a desire for ceremony and symbolic interaction. Our daily social interactions include several ritualistic elements such as hand-shaking; bowing; and collective behaviors such as birthday celebrations, weddings, etc. All ritual carries a transcendent dimension, veering toward religious expression, as witnessed in *rites of passage* throughout ancient and modern cultures. Sacraments are the Christian equivalent of such rites.

Today, religious devotion endures a sustained attack from several quarters. Christian churches either endorse inherited devotional practices—especially around symbols like the Cross—with few attempts to update the expression or understand the deeper motivation, or, alternatively, the churches discourage such devotions in favor of more formal liturgy and worship. Social scientists tend to be forthrightly dismissive and strongly condemnatory of devotional practices. Some dismiss popular devotions as psychological props related to primitive instinct; inherited and unreflective forms of immaturity and codependency, Darwinian-based evocations to cope with new evolutionary challenges, and conjuring acts of the human brain (brain science). Such critical observations are necessary to responsible discernment, and alert us to deviations that can, and do, arise, but in our current rationalistic culture, such explanations are often given an exaggerated importance.

Exonerating suffering for the sake of suffering (as in the Mel Gibson movie, *The Passion of the Christ*) is rarely a healthy or wholesome thing to do; nor was it ever intended as a faith practice by the historical Jesus. It has been strongly endorsed by traditional devotional religion all over the world. In the Christian context, the crucifix is an evocative emblem providing comfort and consolation for millions of marginalized and oppressed people. Christian leaders have inadvertently—and sometimes deliberately—used this devotion to reinforce domination and control.

By reminding people consistently of their sins and unworthiness—the suffering incurred as a result—it is much easier to exert influence over them. These are just some of the dysfunctionalities associated with misguided devotionalism. These aberrations need to be addressed, corrected, and in several cases, abandoned—while acknowledging their necessity, on a temporary basis, for those incarcerated in the culture of poverty and oppression.

The correlation between poverty and religious devotion is very high and has been observed on a universal scale. God and religion remain hugely important for people condemned to oppression and a degrading existence. Few can deny the unhealthy dependency at work here, and yet, we cannot readily dismiss such codependency because, without it, millions of outsiders would succumb to despair and nihilism. Religion may be the opium of the people in the sense that it provides hope against overwhelming odds, and indeed it is this survival function that has guaranteed the triumph of religion itself. It is precisely when living conditions improve that we often note people outliving the need for religion.

The Spirituality of Liberation

The Cross was never intended to be an end in itself. It is a cruel barbaric symbol that has nothing to do with God's love, with salvation, or with redemption. Jesus was pushed onto a Cross, and killed, precisely because he tried to rid the world of his day of all meaningless suffering that prevailed amid torture, pain, and oppression. Instead of imitating his suffering (which he never sought or intended) we should be striving to emulate his prophetic courage and his passion for a world characterized by justice, freedom and new hope. This is the vision encapsulated in the notion of *The Spirituality of Liberation*.

This brings us to the critical and catalytic role of the outsider and right to the heart of Christian faith itself. There are good psychological, social, and ritual reasons why people need devotions and forums for creative expression. To get rid of devotions completely would erode the mystical core of human meaning. How to channel the capacity for devotion into more responsible and creative religion is a major challenge of our time. And this also evokes a new threshold for the liberation of the outsider.

Suffering seems to be part and parcel of the human condition, a demise that neither the secular nor religious culture is capable of rectifying in any substantial or enduring way. In religious terms, original sin (variously named) is the foundational culprit; secular forces often invoke the Darwinian struggle involved in the survival of the fittest. Both theories provide anthropocentric, short-sighted explanations. When we look at creation in its cosmic and planetary dimensions, we readily note an enduring paradox of creation-cum-destruction. This is not a *flaw*, but rather a *paradox* that seems to be essential to the flourishing of creation at large and to every life-form within it. I have explored its meaning in other works (O'Murchu 2002, 2011, 2012) and will not repeat the arguments here.

If we attempt to get rid of the paradox, we end up destroying ourselves and everything around us. *The paradox is essential* to the well-being and evolution of creation. It does involve suffering, pain, and destruction, but such suffering is better understood as negative fallout endowed with purpose. From the human point of view, therefore, the critical question becomes "*What is the suffering that may be described as meaningful* (in the sense that is necessary for the flourishing of creation) *and what causes other forms of suffering to be meaningless?*" The daunting truth confronting humanity today is that most of the meaningless suffering we witness within and around us is actually caused by humans themselves. And instead of waiting for some divine Savior to rescue us from such meaningless suffering, as adult people of faith, we are slowly realizing that it is up to humanity itself to activate the redemption. It is we who have created the mess; let's grow up (as God and Jesus want us to do) and seek to resolve the destruction we cause either directly or indirectly.

Consequently, the spirituality of liberation focuses attention on the quality and quantity of suffering that are innate to releasing and empowering life's greater potential: "I have come that they may have life and have it to the full" (John 10:10). It rejects the notion of suffering being valuable as an end in itself. To the contrary, it seeks the abolition of all meaningless suffering in the world, on the conviction that God and Jesus sought that outcome. The spirituality of liberation works on two fronts:

1. To address the extensive ignorance humans have adopted in the face of extensive suffering; this is a kind of self-inflected delusion propagated in large measure by imperial religion as a tactic to keep people subdued and passive.

2. To explore and highlight how humans need to become proactive in ridding the world of meaningless suffering instead of waiting—in codependent fashion—for a divine rescuer to do it for them. In this context, Jesus is understood as the primordial exemplar of one who set out to rid the world of all meaningless pain and suffering.

First, a shift in consciousness needs to happen, to alert us to the ignorance in which we are ensnared and to take steps to rise above it. Much of the meaningless suffering all around us relates to the following factors:

1. Our ignorance of creation's great paradox of creation-cum-destruction results in humans repeating the destructive behaviors that only we ourselves can change and outgrow.

2. Our several manipulations whereby we try to change and modify the paradox to suit human ends, over against the larger creation, contribute significantly to the meaninglessness of human suffering.

3. Our objectification of the surrounding creation, whereby we treat the web of life in a materialistic and mechanistic way, contributes much to meaningless suffering.

4. Many diseases and illnesses are the result of lifestyles, at variance with the well-being of humans and that of other life-forms sharing the planet with us.

5. Our human constructs governing politics, economics, social policy, medicine, and education all contribute to meaningless suffering in the world, mainly because all such constructs are poisoned by the anthropocentric desire for power and domination.

6. We have deviously interpreted the Christian story of the Cross (redemption and salvation) to validate and rationalize the meaningless suffering caused primarily by ourselves. We then expect God and Jesus to rescue us from the mess that we ourselves have created.

Second, we need to redirect our creative energy to assuming proactive coresponsibility for the meaningless suffering that prevails. We need to discern its causes and mobilize our collective resources to remedy its destructive impact, all of which will require a massive change of outlook for a species still immersed in the patriarchal delusion of divide and conquer. Among other things, it requires a radical shift from our codependent religiosity. There will be no divine rescue because it is not God's problem in the first place—a truth often obfuscated by misplaced devotionalism. Jesus did not die on the Cross to rescue us from sin or wrongdoing, a convoluted myth based on the flawed theory of original sin.

Jesus was killed because his radical new vision of the Companionship of Empowerment set in motion a process of liberation in which people would become more adult and thus begin to address and rectify the abuse of human power, the primary source of most of the meaningless suffering in the world. And this process of liberation and empowerment would seriously undermine the dysfunctional power games of those who crucified Jesus. Exposing and unmasking such powers became intolerable for the "insiders" of his day, those who held the power and were determined to hold on to it. Jesus became the scapegoat of the threatened powers and was promptly executed.

In a word, Jesus set in motion *a nonviolent spirituality of liberation*. He alerted people to the myopic stupidity of the culture of patriarchal domination, privileging the few insiders over against the massive number of disempowered outsiders. He chose to become an outsider himself, to catalyze for all outsiders (victims):

1. An awareness that things need not be this way;
2. That God never intended things to be this way; and
3. That inclusive freedom is God's desire for all, a dream archetypally rooted in the Companionship of Empowerment.

Like other prophetic figures, Jesus paid the ultimate price. And the dream for which Jesus lived and died still awaits its fuller realization, not something that can be achieved by the violent power of the Cross, but by humans who have yet to learn how to cocreate with Jesus in a nonviolent way.

A False Spirituality

A major stumbling block for Christians—over many centuries—is our tendency to overspiritualize the Cross itself. This is also a dysfunctional strategy of ecclesiastical insiders—another subtle trick to delude naive followers into submissive obedience. A great deal of Christian rhetoric is devoted to the *love* Jesus shows by dying for us on the Cross. The death is portrayed as a supreme act of love, pure agape. Elaborate commentaries then emphasize the need to embrace suffering in order to love as Jesus loved. The more we love, the more we suffer. Love comes with a price, and it is the price worth paying on the pathway to holiness where we grow deeper into God's love.

This is a deceptively naive and dangerous rhetoric of a love so sentimentalized and convoluted that it contradicts the authentic meaning of love itself. There is no love associated with the brutality of Calvary, nor is there any justice! God did not hand over his beloved son to die for sinful humanity—a medieval, feudal proposal dangerously verging on child abuse and frequently used throughout history to foster victimization. The death of Jesus is the product of institutional violence, scapegoating the prophet who unflinchingly honored the spirituality of liberation, to break down the barrier between insiders and outsiders, and re-create the human family as one (hence the notion of at-one-ment). It is in the power of this unity—to bring in excluded outsiders—that humanity is empowered afresh to engage—in a more responsible and creative way—the great paradox of creation at large. This is the only long-term resolution to the meaningless suffering humanity has endured for far too long.

Chapter 10

The Women Who Threatened Patriarchy

The historical sources are simply too contradictory and simultaneously too silent on the matter.

— Jeffrey Kripal

Women's prominence did not, however, go unchallenged. Every variety of ancient Christianity that advocated the legitimacy of women's leadership was eventually declared heretical, and evidence of women's early leadership roles was erased or suppressed.

— Karen King

Two thousand years on, it is impossible to determine with any degree of accuracy how women fared in the time of Jesus and how they contributed to the emergence of early Christianity. In fact, the subject received scant attention before the middle of the twentieth century, gathering thereafter a substantial amount of research and discernment.

143

Although objective historical data is difficult to come by, we can reconstruct in broad strokes women's participation in social life and religious practice. Insights from the social sciences, reinforced by archaeological findings provide significant information. While the dominant Greek influence relegated women to second-class status, mainly within domestic roles related to child rearing and home maintenance, research increasingly provides supplementary evidence for situations where women played proactive and participative roles as well.

How Jesus himself, and Christian leaders like St. Paul, regarded women is quite a complex issue. Contemporary feminist writers tend to view Jesus as inclusive and affirmative of women above and beyond the cultural norms of the day, despite some glaring examples of misogynist dismissal, as in Matthew 21:31 where Jesus seems to concur with the derogatory naming of women as whores (harlots) or the story of the Syrophoenician woman, dismissed because of her lowly Gentile status (Mark 7:24–30). In dealing with Gospel material, it is impossible to distinguish what belongs to Jesus himself and what was imposed by the views of the evangelists who composed the Gospels.

The Pauline evidence seems to be easier to discern, thanks to the contemporary distinction between the original Paul and caricatures of Paul in letters attributed to him, but not necessarily written by him—a journalistic strategy that seems to have been common at the time. According to the insightful research of Borg and Crossan (2009), the Pauline writings fall into three categories, effectively portraying three Pauls rather than one. The first Paul seems to have been a radical visionary for inclusive empowerment and communal liberation, and we encounter him in the letter to the Romans, 1 and 2 Corinthians, 1 Thessalonians, Galatians, Philippians, and Philemon. The second Paul is a much more conservative character encouraging slaves to obey their masters and wives to be subject to their husbands—in the disputed letters of Ephesians, Colossians and 2 Thessalonians.

The third is the reactionary Paul of 1 and 2 Timothy and Titus, tamed and co-opted by the values of the imperial culture, and particularly dismissive of, and negative toward, women in the earliest Christian communities.

Women in the Gospels

Although rarely named in the Gospels, it does appear that women participated in the following of Jesus as codisciples. Elizabeth Schussler Fiorenza (1983) argues vehemently for a discipleship of equals, a conviction for which it is difficult to mobilize substantial verification. There are a number of hints that women played a more domestic role providing for the practical needs of Jesus and the disciples. Some scholars suggest that some of the male disciples may have been accompanied by their wives, and alongside pairs of brothers, pairs of sisters might well have functioned in the work of evangelization, e.g., Martha and Mary, as proposed by Warren Carter (1996) and further explored by Mary Stormer Hanson (2013). Occasionally we glimpse strong female characters, who not only defy the subservient role, but exhibit convictions of faith comparable to the best male witness evidenced in the Gospels—the already named Syrophoenician woman, the woman confronting the unjust judge, the Samaritan woman.

When it comes to women's significance in the Gospels, the most impressive evidence comes toward the end of Jesus' life as the women hang in there, while all the males flee in fear. Here the women exhibit a quality of fidelity that seems unique and praiseworthy, and arguably has not been given the inclusive significance it deserves or the serious discernment that it deserves.

Most of the material in this chapter will be devoted to Gospel female characters who serve as catalysts for the Gospel inclusivity being explored in the present work. To furnish a more comprehensive picture of women—and their inclusion—in the New Testament generally, I'll briefly outline women's significance in the Pauline literature.

Women in the Pauline Writings

References to women in Paul's writings are unevenly distributed, with almost two-thirds occurring in Romans 16. Without this chapter, our knowledge of the ways in which women functioned in the early church would be quite sparse, at least as far as the biblical record is concerned.

References to women in Paul's remaining letters are either entirely absent or very sporadic. The only women mentioned outside of Romans 16 are Chloe and Priscilla (1 Cor.), Euodia and Syntyche (Phil.), Nympha (Col.), Apphia (Philem.), and Claudia and Priscilla (2 Tim.). Since the references to Chloe and to Euodia and Syntyche are somewhat incidental, and virtually no information is given concerning the other women mentioned outside of Romans 16 (Nympha, Apphia, Claudia), Priscilla alone commands more reliable historical investigation.

Of the persons mentioned in relation to the Pauline mission in the apostle's writings, 82 percent are men and 18 percent are women. Once multiple references are eliminated, the Pauline epistles identify about fifty-five men by name, associated with Paul in mission, compared with *seventeen* women.

Priscilla and Aquila: Nevertheless, according to the book of Acts and Paul's epistles, Priscilla and Aquila were among Paul's most strategic allies in his Gentile mission supporting his endeavors in such major centers as Ephesus, Corinth, and Rome. Together they hosted house churches in their home wherever they went, instructed others such as Apollos, and even "risked their necks" for Paul (cf. Rom. 16:4).

Phoebe: As a wealthy woman, a benefactress or patroness, Phoebe would have used her financial means to come to the aid of others, especially foreigners, by providing housing and financial aid, and by representing their interests before local authorities. This would have been a needed ministry in a busy seaport such as Cenchrea. Phoebe, then, was probably a woman of high social standing and some wealth, who put her status, resources, and time at the services of traveling Christians, like Paul, who needed help and support. Much more significantly, according to Romans 16:1, it is the same Phoebe who is entrusted to carry the Letter of Romans to Rome. In this capacity, she would have to read the letter in various assemblies in Rome, preach on it, and explain its contents. Was Phoebe also a woman with a quality of learning far in excess of social expectations of her time? More significantly, how many more learned women of her caliber were involved in early Christian ministry?

Junia and Andronicus: Moreover, Andronicus and Junia are identified as well known (notorious according to one translation) among the apostles. Scholars debate whether we are dealing with a narrow or broad sense of apostleship. Perhaps at the time, apostleship did not have the specific meaning it later assumed, and therefore a designation like traveling missionary might be more accurate. Among contemporary scholars, Andronicus and Junia tend to be regarded as husband and wife, probably from a wealthy background, and gave of their resources generously to support the missionary endeavor. Although some question if Junia actually refers to a woman, many endorse the evidence accumulated by Rena Pederson (2006), suggesting that she was an outstanding female *apostolos* in the early church.

Apart from *Thecla*, it seems that none of the women mentioned in relation to the Pauline mission serves as pastor-teacher or elder. Phoebe apparently functioned as a deaconess and is also called benefactress. If Junia was a woman (which is highly probable), she probably served as an itinerant missionary or, less likely, as a messenger, together with her presumed husband, Andronicus. Priscilla, together with her husband Aquila, had a church meeting in her house, as did *Nympha* and *Apphia* (with Philemon). The suggestion that Thecla might have been a significant Church leader and pastor of equal standing with Paul (see Hylen 2014) is confirmed by archeological evidence outlined by

Crossan and Reed (2004). The positions of *Euodia* and *Syntyche* in the Philippian church were apparently significant enough to threaten the unity of the entire congregation. These two women were (in all probability) counted among Paul's co-workers during his stay at Philippi.

In the ministries of both Jesus and Paul, men bore the ultimate responsibility for the ongoing mission, with women actively supporting and contributing to that undertaking. It is often suggested that Paul taught that women were not to serve as pastor-teachers or elders, and the evidence cited tends to be from the Pastoral Epistles, which today are considered not to have been written by Paul himself. Women also supported the Pauline mission by exercising numerous other ministries.

Women Found a Way In

In seeking to retrieve an inclusive significance for women in the Gospels, first, Elizabeth Schussler Fiorenza (1983, 2001) recommends that we adopt both a double hermeneutic of suspicion and remembrance. We need to surface and name the several patriarchal forces that sought to keep women excluded, marginalized, and disempowered.

Second, we need to access the subverted memory by which women continued to claim a voice against the oppressive forces of previous times, and re-member (put back together) a subverted wisdom that has been subverted and fragmented. In that way, we can lay fresh foundations upon which we can reconstruct a more inclusive and empowering sense of mission, one that reclaims a more authentic past and a more promising future—for women and men alike!

I would like to add a third strategy, which we might name as a hermeneutic of archetypal wisdom. It has much in common with the hermeneutic of remembrance but strives to delve deeper into the subversive, creative imagination witnessed in situations of cultural and human oppression in every age. This unconquerable hunger for freedom can be detected in the yearnings and aspirations that embolden fables and stories that endure. While we cannot identify solid historical fact for such narratives, we can discern a subversive, empowering wisdom, which evokes truths and possibilities that evoke and awaken deep values. Among such values, is that unique quality of inclusivity described throughout the pages of this book.

Prose is a limited resource for the release or expression of archetypal truth. An artistic expression is needed to uncover that which has been hidden and suppressed for so long, to illuminate meaning endowed with a transrational significance, and to express afresh a message that carries enduring hope now and for the future. The creative resource I am most acquainted with is that of poetry. I will employ poetic imagination to engage with four Gospel women, each of whom, it seems to me, is imbued richly with archetypal wisdom. And in each case is an unambiguous desire for a newly empowering inclusivity.

Beyond the Jaundiced Eye (Luke 7:36-50)

In one of the more memorable stories from Luke's Gospel, a Pharisee, named Simon invites Jesus to his house to share a meal. While at table a woman of disrepute brought an alabaster jar of ointment and began to wash the feet of Jesus with both her tears and the ointment, proceeding to wipe his feet with her hair. Annoyed by what was happening, Simon began to object that a woman of such disrepute should even be touching Jesus. Challenging his judgmental stance, Jesus highlights the virtue of forgiveness and then confronts Simon with a piercing question: "Simon, do you see this woman?" (Luke 7:44). Taking the liberty to paraphrase, the question may be heard as follows: "Simon, do you actually see the female person standing in front of you? Are you so blinded by moralistic judgments that you are no longer capable of seeing this person for who she really is? And if you cannot even see her, then what hope is there that you will ever be able to include her—either in your heart or in your home!"

Many feminists highlight the cruel invisibility to which women have been subjected under a range of patriarchal regimes. Oppression in itself was not the problem; worse still was the exclusion whereby the dominant male culture chose not to see, did not want to see, and added injury to insult by not even registering the very presence of a woman. This is the issue being addressed in how Jesus confronts and challenges Simon. And the depth and power of the encounter is best captivated in poetic rendition.

Simon, Can You See?

Can you see this person standing here, a woman of full truth
With the elegance of womanhood, richly feminine imbued?
With the beauty of her passion, erotic to the core
And the birthing-power within her inviting to explore!
Simon, can you see? Can you see? Can you see?

Can you see the tears of centuries of patriarchal woe
And the courage it must take her for integrity of soul?
Can you see the waves of flowing hair with which she wiped
      my feet
And the kisses of her intimacy, making healing so replete?
Simon, can you see? . . .

Can you see her hospitality, her warmth, her embrace;
Her ability for birthing as a mother to each race?
A living icon of the ages, the Goddess we long have known,
Maligned and desecrated by the dogmas YOU have sown!
Simon, can you see? . . .

Can you see her jar of ointment, anointing to empower
Those excluded by oppression, overwhelmed and weighed
      down?
Can you see her gracious pouring out, abundant as of yore

While you stand there in judgment, a pontificating bore!
Simon, can you see? . . .

Her eyes though filled with weeping tears are contemplating
    clear.
She can see right through the lot of us, our judgments and
    our fear.
Remember Holy Wisdom—she embodies it anew
And she radiates sheer goodness for creation to imbue!
Simon, can you see? . . .

She has known the ups and downs of life, the sinful and the
    free.
And forgiven much, she's loving much—for empowering
    liberty.
The system can't contain her and the freedom she proclaims,
She's a living revelation where love and justice reigns.
Simon, can you see? . . .

Long after we have run our course and echoes fade in time
Her name will be invoked afresh in Scripture and in rhyme.
And the alabaster jar she holds will replenish many souls,
And where the Gospel is proclaimed, her fame will be
    disclosed.
And, then, Simon, you might see; I hope you will see!

The invisibility so endemic to patriarchy has been heavily
buttressed by formal religion, particularly by the monotheistic
faiths. Christianity holds an appalling record of misogynist degradation, remnants of which still endure in various denominations and churches. It is an exclusion that can never be justified
in the name of Gospel integrity. To the contrary, the inclusivity
being explored in the present work declares unambiguously that
women belong fully to the Companionship of Empowerment;

indeed, they are indispensable witnesses to its promised hope and liberation.

The Archetypal Coming of Age
(Mark 5:24-34; Luke 8:43-48; Matt. 9:20-22)

The story of the daughter of Jairus is one of the most underrated parables in Gospel lore. Widely considered to be a literal raising of a dead person to life, all the symbolic and archetypal infrastructure is either ignored or misinterpreted. We are told that the girl is *twelve years old,* and the two parts of her story are bridged by the narrative of the woman with the hemorrhage focused also on the figure twelve.

At the time of Jesus, a girl's twelfth birthday was the cultural signal for the onset of her fertility, marked by her first menstruation. In the misogynist culture of the day, this was read as her readiness for the procreative process, initiated by finding a young male to whom she would be betrothed and to whom she would be married, often by her fifteenth birthday. The younger she is married, the better her chances to produce healthy offspring for her male consort.

Let's be clear about the anthropology: males are full human beings who can reproduce in the power of the seed. Females are essentially biological organisms created by God for one primary purpose, namely, to produce offspring. In other words, women are not full human beings (following Aristotle, Thomas Aquinas described woman as *misbegotten males*). Consequently, when we are told that the girl is sick—and later dead—are we dealing with some bizarre coded language that paradoxically alerts us to a subverted truth?

Here we are encountering a young, sexual, fertile, beautiful girl, embarking on the wonder of her womanhood, yet everything transpiring in her life according to God's creativity is demonized and reduced to crude biology.[1] In parabolic terms, one is forced to ask, "Who or what is sick? The girl or her perverse culture?"

And later in the story when she is described as being dead, ironically that is the truth, in the sense that everything unique and sacred about her coming-of-age is condemned to death in that highly misogynist culture.

Once again the climax to the parabolic miracle is probably in that face-to-face encounter between Jesus and the girl alleged to be dead. "Talitha cumi . . . —arise and take your place in the world as a wonderful, sexual, human being, as God and the universe desires you to be." The last sentence in the story may be crucial evidence for the interpretation adopted here: "He told her parents to give her something to eat" (Mark 5:43b). Let's assume that Jesus had been speaking in Aramaic when he addressed the young woman. Let's try and hear him out as he also addresses her parents not with a flat Greek statement that she should be given some food (because she is so weak), but with an empowering inclusive Aramaic challenge, loaded with prophetic intent: "Whether menstruating or not, you include her fully at your family table, and you dare never again exclude her."

The daughter of Jairus serves as a vivid archetype for every woman (and indirectly, for every person, male or female). To literalize her story does her—and all of us—a grave injustice. Her story is an empowering parable, unmasking some of the most cruel and sinister dynamics that undermine human dignity—and particularly that of women—even to our own day. Hers is a story with an enduring archetypal truth, which the following poem helps to illuminate:

The Daughter of Jairus Speaks Up!

I'm known as the daughter of Jairus,
please call me Rebecca by name
And my mother is never referred to,
condemned in anonymous fame.
Well let's get priorities sorted

In a culture with so much distorted;
With women's uniqueness aborted,
In the name of divine platitude.
To bring me back to life in the Gospels—
is a farce I'll no longer endure.
I never was dead in the first place
except in the patriarch's lore.

At twelve years of age we young women,
 our bodies erotic exult,
And we shed what is crimson and wholesome,
our breakthrough into the adult.
In the eyes of the dominant culture,
With the stare of a hot phallic vulture,
Reproducing with hope for the future
In the name of divine platitude.
It's only biology matters,
for women are objects of lust,
Except when the sons are begotten,
begrudgingly we earn some trust.

So, the Gospels are right in declaring
that I am effectively dead,
For everything sacred about me
is condemned in this culture of dread.
I'm fertile and sexual, embodied,
God's blood and new life is not sullied,
And my womanhood will not be buried
In the name of divine platitude.
Empowered by the message of Jesus,
I'll rise to my true dignity,
And break through misogynist silence,
in the dream of a new liberty.

There's nothing unclean in my body,
and no need to drench me all pure,
It's all in the plan of creation,
a wisdom that's sure to endure.
And no need to shield me from contact,
Please touch me and hold me as subject!
And get rid of the norms that impact
In the name of divine platitude.
To the family table you bring me,
in the gift of the fullest embrace
Even if I am menstruating,
it's all in the power of God's grace.

And please call me by name as Rebecca,
A daughter of Goddess so true,
An archetype thirteen remembers
My life and my blood will renew!

The Fierce Awakening of Feminine Self-empowerment

The story of the woman with the hemorrhage is one of the most memorable of Gospel stories, made all the more intriguing by Mark's *intercalating* placing of the story between split segments of the narrative of Jairus' daughter. (This is a literary device frequently used by Mark.) Clearly there is a play on the figure twelve, the age at which the young girl is considered to be a biologically productive person and in the case of the woman with the persistent bleeding, marking a long period of time. In both cases, we are looking at oppressive exclusion linked with body fluids, in this case, blood. The complex portrayal of the daughter of Jairus has already been reviewed.

It does not take too much imagination to envisage the plight of the woman who has long endured exclusion, oppression, slander, and demoralization. Not only did the woman have to overcome discouragement in order to reach out, she also had to overcome inferiority, shame, and feelings of worthlessness. Since the Jewish religious leaders considered women to be ceremonially unclean during their monthly periods (when they were bleeding), the woman had the added shame of always feeling unclean because her gynecological disorder caused constant bleeding. As someone who was considered to be unclean, the woman couldn't worship in the synagogue or enjoy normal social relationships (anyone who touched her while she was bleeding was also considered unclean, so people likely avoided her).

Moralists would have harshly judged her; legalists would have condemned her; doctors apparently gave up on her; neighbors would probably make her the subject of slanderous gossip, wondering if it was her own sins or those of her ancestors that caused her to suffer this terrible curse. Among Gospel people condemned to being outsiders, she must surely be the epitome.

Afflicted with such huge rejection and denunciation, we would expect her (at least occasionally) to be suffering from severe depression. In such a state, her sense of personal motivation would be very low, barely surviving from one day to the next. If somebody drew her attention to a renowned healer in the vicinity, she probably would not have the energy or willpower to consider positively the option being offered. Moreover, her sense of unworthiness would make it very difficult for her to show any zeal or enthusiasm.

Yet, that is exactly what does happen! Against all odds, she makes an eager, assertive response, and of her own initiative (it seems) she makes a beeline for Jesus who, according to Luke (8:42), has a crowd crushing around him. Yet, she gets right through to where Jesus is and grabs his cloak from behind as if a residual unworthiness restrains her from approaching him face to face.

What is this *fierce awakening* that caught up with her? We will never know its precise source, but one does wonder if this is not a reminder that our engagement with the Companionship of

Empowerment (the Kingdom) requires a degree of self-empowerment to respond authentically. And having made the initial effort, it looks like a reckless freedom can carry us forward. The woman makes her way through the dense crowd determined that nothing or nobody will hinder her. This is supposed to be a broken, depressed woman—where did she get that incredible resilience from? And as she goes through the crowd she is obviously rubbing shoulders with many people—automatically making them all ritually impure. Is she doing it deliberately? *Has the New Reign of God caught up with her to a degree that she does not give a damn about rules or regulations anymore?* She desires but one thing, and—worthy or unworthy—she is going wholeheartedly for it.

And then comes what is widely regarded as the miracle! Jesus' query on who touched him is probably an editorial gloss that need not detain us. What is more likely to have transpired was an encounter of archetypal significance, which then becomes the miracle. Jesus turns around and looks the woman straight in the eye (probably the first time she will ever have had this experience) and with a gaze of pure compassion—unadulterated love—something subliminal shifts within her and she knows a quality of transformation that will transform her plight for evermore. We need to be wary of the "nice" ending to many of the miracle stories in the Gospels—indicating that her bleeding stopped. In this case, the bleeding may not have ceased, but such was the transformation that took place within her; it is quite secondary whether the bleeding ceased or not. As a wounded healer from here on, it might make more archetypal sense to suggest that the bleeding did not cease. The miracle in question is at a much deeper level.

I want to suggest it is a process-type miracle rather than a single event. The miracle begins in the fierce awakening whereby she decided in the first place that she was going to approach Jesus. *It is the disempowered outsider who initiates the miracle process*. It continues in the fierce determination to reach Jesus despite the crowd. It subverts all the prohibitions around ritual purity. And, finally, is the climax in the face-to-face encounter between the woman and Jesus. If words were spoken by Jesus, which is likely to be the case, then this is the likely gist: "Even though you are a woman with an unfortunate bleeding condition, you are nonetheless a full person before God and before the world. Rise above your plight and get on with your life!" It is not some miraculous words that seal the miracle; it is the compassionate gaze as the core ingredient of the archetypal encounter.

Prose cannot hope to capture the sheer depth and pathos of this encounter. We are into mystical, archetypal territory in which poetry offers a more empowering option to discern the truth radiates before our eyes.

The Wounded Healer Speaks Out

'Twas awkward and painful, but worse still 'twas shameful,
This curse I was carrying for so many years.
The clergy denounced me and the doctors renounced me,
While young guys pronounced me a dirty old slag.
I never even realised a power from within.

To the wind I threw caution, fed up with depression
And broke all the rules by joining the crowd.
There were stories of healing which got my head reeling
Through the crowd I was feeling my way to the source.
Determined to awaken my power from within.

My wisdom assured me that a mere touch had cured me.
I clung to his garment as hard as I could.
His gaze it surprised me as wholeness now seized me,
I stood mesmerized that 'twould happen to me.
Enamored and blessed by a power from within.

His words were not many, but his eyes were uncanny
Right into my heart came the gaze of true peace.
What a load he had lifted, what hope he had shifted,
And the healing he gifted I'll never forget.
So much was achieved through the power from within.

The healer that's wounded can now remain grounded
And undo oppression against mighty odds.
And you that are wounded must never be hounded
By people confounded inflicting your pain.
Like me, you can call forth the power from within.

Straight in the Eye!

Next, comes the story recorded in Luke 13:10–17 of a woman bent over for eighteen years (see commentary by Dr. Ralph F. Wilson: www.Jesuswalk.com/lessons/13_10–17.htm). Medically, this disease is probably what physician's today would call Ankylosing Spondylitis, or Marie-Strümpell Disease, a fusion of the spinal bones, a chronic progressive form of arthritis distinguished by inflammation and stiffness—and in some patients even ossification of joints—especially in the lower spine. Even today it is a difficult condition to treat.

Early in the course of the disease, sufferers often find that the pain is relieved somewhat when they lean forward. The more they lean in order to relieve the pain, the greater the angle, until a patient might be bent almost double, as seems to be the case with the woman in this story. We are told that her disease had been progressing for eighteen years. She is bound with invisible chains, chains of calcium now hardened in her spine, an affliction attributed to an evil spirit according to Luke. This would have been a popular understanding at the time of Jesus; many sicknesses were attributed to adverse spiritual influences. What today we identify as *internalized oppression* is probably the underlying etiology in many of the bodily deprivations alluded to in the Gospels.

The astute analysis of British Scripture scholar Louise Lawrence (2013) illuminates the stigma and oppression accompanying may body deformities in the time of Jesus.

Luke uses the story to highlight the confrontation around Sabbath observance, and the creative freedom with which Jesus circumvents the prevailing legalities in order to restore the woman's health and thus reintegrate her with the community. Are we therefore, looking at an allegory around Sabbath observance/transgression and, if so, what might the story signify in its original context? If this miracle is viewed as a parable in action, what might the daring new vision entail? We note in Luke 13:14 that the synagogue president is "indignant because Jesus had healed on the Sabbath," but instead of confronting Jesus, he seems to blame the people for digressing from the Sabbath regulations. And one wonders how he feels about the woman now restored to the fullness of her well-being. Now standing straight, she can look him in the eye, and he cannot avoid her gaze as he could have done while she was bent over.

During her eighteen long years of deformity and oppression, she must often have felt broken and beaten down in a state of painful agony. Children would make fun of her. Her husband might have rejected her. Self-righteous people would gossip on what curse might have caused her affliction. And one wonders was she a nonperson even for the medics of the day?

And now she's standing upright in front of the gathered worshippers, who amazingly seem pleased about her new-found freedom. *And she looks the president straight in the eye*, a challenging gaze he cannot avoid. And alas, he can only respond by ranting on about Sabbath regulations. He cannot handle the release of Gospel empowerment, and the one he would rather keep outside, is now right there in front of his eyes. *He cannot exclude her anymore.* Poetry captivates beautifully the dramatic impact of the encounter:

Standing Up Straight!

They thought 'twas the spirits inflicted her pain
With posture distorted she moved with great strain.
Bent over by burden for eighteen long years,
With anguish and struggle, and crippled by fear.
To stand straight again, being a woman in sin,
Was a dream she had never imagined!
And the culture of judgment she could not escape,
Some curse from the past they alleged for her fate.
So crushed in her spirit by a faith quite corrupt,
It took courage defiant to hold her chin up.
To stand straight again, in a culture of sin,
Was a dream she had never imagined.

And Jesus saw through the distortions so false,
A daughter of Abraham, she, too, had her place.
An equal in status to whatever the force,
And he called forth the freedom to dislodge her curse.
To stand straight again, in spite of her sin,
Was a dream she had never imagined.

The Spirit of life and the Spirit that heals,
Is the first touch of God to free and release.
The forces that bind through shame, guilt and fear,
Will never outdo God's freedom so clear.
To stand straight again, and outgrow her sin,
Was a dream she had never imagined.

But the Synagogue boss with his righteous acclaim,
Felt his power undermined by this freedom regained.
And a Sabbath good deed, it angered his soul,
While, in fact, he's annoyed by a woman made whole.

To stand straight again, in spite of her sin,
Was a dream that HE never imagined.

When a woman stands straight with truth in her eye,
She poses a threat to all forces on high.
Subdued they would keep her—she should know her place,
But the New Reign of God has drawn a fresh trace.
To stand straight again, released of her sin,
Is a dream for us all to imagine.

She stands in her place, her body aglow.
She raises her voice with the wisdom to know
That freedom begets a new option to grow,
With oppression declared to rule us no more.
To stand straight again, oppression upend,
Is the task for us all to imagine.

Women Arising!

Of all the Gospel material related to women none, is more enigmatic and empowering than the role of the women in post-Resurrection space. In Chapter 9, I alluded briefly to the women on Calvary remaining faithful to the end. For those women, it was anything but an end. Even when the male disciples fled in fear, they remained to await a new frightening dawn that would propel them into a mission transcending all other missionary endeavors recorded in Gospel lore. The early church seemed unprepared for the archetypal breakthrough and proceeded to consign the women to historical invisibility.

The archetypal depth of this transition from the devastation of Calvary, through the dark dawn of Easter morn (according to all the Gospels, the women were filled with *fear*), to an unprecedented missionary breakthrough is a process the rational mind will never be able to comprehend. It marks what might well be the greatest paradigm shift noted anywhere in the Gospels! When all is doomed to ultimate despair, hope lingers on painfully and poignantly in a marginalized group led by Mary Magdalene. Poetry releases the Spirit-filled initiative, the parabolic truth Christianity has long suppressed, one that in all probability will eventually come back to haunt our petrified imaginations.

Risen Empowerment

What happened to Jesus on the first Easter Day
Is a myst'ry beyond comprehension.
The lure of another dimension.
A boundary-breaker we cannot contain,
A creative disruption we cannot explain.
The heart that is silent, mid echoes endure
Must live with a mystery both subtle and pure.
Empowering a new transformation.

What happened the women on the first Easter Day
Breaks open a daring horizon,
Inviting all hearts to discern.
Mid the grieving and trauma of loss,
The horror to stand at the foot of a Cross.
A body we think was buried in haste,
And a tomb that was empty but restless in taste.
Empowering a strange group of women.

What happened to the twelve on the first Easter Day
Is betrayal of a fearful desertion,
Lest they too endure crucifixion.
While Peter clings on by the skin of his teeth,
And Thomas is searching for holes in the feet.
The others are nowhere to be seen or heard,
As opaque as they are in the Gospel's own word.
Not much use for Gospel empowerment!

What happened to those on the first Easter Day,
whose witness is rare and transgressive?
With wisdom so bold and decisive.
They remember the echo of words that endure
As they pierce the dark vale with hope to secure.
"We know he's alive where faith can perceive,
A depth to endure beyond space-time retrieve."
Empowering a radical breakthrough.

What happened to those on the first Day of Easter,
The faithful disciples by Magdalene led?
A subverted truth the patriarchs dread.
Beyond all the theories that time has construed,
Beyond the oppression we have too long endured.
The first ones commissioned for Easter proclaim
A woman-led mission we've brutally maimed.
But we can't keep subverting empowerment.

Resurrection still flourishes and always it will,
Imbued with a truth that time will fulfil.
What women empowered at the dawning breakthrough
will bear fruit in season
despite all the treason.
'Cos justice will render what deserves to endure.

Centuries of misogynist oppression have ensued, and justice
is still waiting to be done. Not until the women—who were so
committed to Gospel inclusivity—are themselves included will
the Christian conscience be at peace. Nor will the Christian faith
community really know what empowering ministry looks like,
with its paradigmatic impact for church and world alike.

And if we are ever to take Gospel inclusivity seriously, how
we regard and embrace the Gospel women is likely to define how

we handle all other residues of patriarchal exclusion. In several aspects of modern life, bold efforts continue to include women as fully as possible in workplaces, government, and in some religious spheres. In many cases, women are elevated to status long attributed to males—particularly in the commercial and economic spheres. Frequently, women end up reinforcing the same patriarchal values they desperately sought to undo. Instead of a new freedom, they are colluding with their ongoing oppression.

Gospel liberation involves a great deal more than this collusive alignment. The Companionship of Empowerment calls us all to a new egalitarian collaboration whereby the uniqueness of both male and female is realized in a way that transcends all social, political, and ecclesiastical co-option. In this regard, the perennial examples of Gospel female initiative are paradigmatic not just for the future of women's liberation, but for the transformation of all humans, male and female alike.

Chapter 11

Pentecost's Queer Outsiders

Ultimately, the relation and legitimization of established authority and power structures weaken the bonds of the religious community and threaten to dissolve the fascination of the original movement.

— WOLFGANG VONDEY

The Bible is not an archetype, an ideal form that sets an unchanging and timeless pattern, but a prototype that is critically open to the possibility of its own transformation.

— ELIZABETH SCHUSSLER FIORENZA

All over the Christian world, Pentecost is a special feast celebrated with great zeal and enthusiasm. Equipped with those proverbial tongues of fire, the apostles were empowered to preach and teach the salvation wrought in the name of the Gospel. Pentecost is considered to be the occasion/event that marks the birth of the church, providing the original missionary mandate launched through those deemed to be the primary followers of the historical Jesus, namely, the twelve apostles. What happened on the first Pentecost is recorded in Acts 2:1–11:

> When Pentecost day came round, all the believers were gathered in one room when suddenly they heard what sounded like a powerful wind from Heaven, the noise of which filled the entire house where they were sitting; and something appeared to them that seemed like tongues of fire; these separated and came to rest on the head of each of them. They were all filled with the Holy Spirit and began to speak foreign languages, as the Spirit gave them the gift of speech. together in one place. Now there were dwelling in Jerusalem Jews, devout people from every nation under heaven. And at this sound the multitude came together, and they were bewildered, because each one heard them speaking in his own native language. "Are not all these who are speaking Galileans?" they asked. How is it that we each hear them in our own native languages? Parthians, Medes and Elamites . . . people from Judea and Cappadocia, Egypt and parts of Libya . . . Visitors from Rome, both Jews and proselytes. We hear them telling in our own tongues the mighty works of God.

This is the central text used each year by all Christian denominations for the liturgies of Pentecost Sunday. There are two parts to this passage. The first is that of Acts 2:1–4, which describes the scene in the Upper Room (cf. Acts 1:12ff.) where the twelve are gathered, with Mary the mother of Jesus in their midst. According earliest Christian belief, articulated particularly through art and legend, the gathered group experienced a kind of mystical transformation in which fiery tongues of flame descended upon each one of them, empowering them with the gift of speech, understood as a divine mandate to go forth to preach and teach the message of the Gospel.

Then there is the second section: Acts 2:5–11, describing a diverse group of ordinary people, from lands that have not yet been evangelized, and these appropriate the impact of what is going on with an unexpected sense of spiritual receptivity. Although the Spirit-filled preachers are using one language, those listening can hear them, each in their own language, and can comprehend the spiritual import as a message that evokes the praise and glory of God. The capacity for this kind of receptivity is generally considered to be an achievement commonly known as *the grace of discernment*, involving deep listening, wise comprehension, and informed spiritual response. According to those versed in the skills of Christian discernment, this is a gifted grace that presumes a deep faith in the living Spirit of God.

Nowhere in the opening chapters of Acts are we told that this second group (in Acts 2:5–11) has been conferred with the gift of the Spirit. According to Acts 2:1–4, that gift has only been given to the twelve preachers. It is from and through the twelve that every other Christian will learn to preach and teach the Gospel. So, how do we make sense of what is going on in this perplexing text? And why is it that in the typical preaching of Pentecost Sunday—all over the Christian world—much attention is given to the first passage (Acts 2:1–4) with scant attention, if any at all, to the second section (Acts 2:5–11)?

Queering Luke's Agenda

I wish to adopt the insights of queer theory to unravel the strange events associated with that first imparting of the Holy Spirit at Pentecost. Traditional biblical exegesis focuses on the privileged gifting of the twelve, and largely, if not totally, ignores what is going on for the other group, described in Acts 2:5–11. Queer theory alerts us to a serious misrepresentation here, another disturbing example, where the outsider holds the critical wisdom, yet is not allowed in to share that wisdom with us.

The term *queer theory* was coined by Teresa de Lauretis at a conference on theorizing lesbian and gay sexualities that was held at the University of California, Santa Cruz in February 1990. Subsequently adopted by a range of scholars, the notion was popularized in works such as Judith Butler's *Gender Trouble*, Eve Kosofsky Sedgwick's *Epistemology of the Closet*, and David Halperin's *One Hundred Years of Homosexuality*.

Although initially inspired by the exclusion and oppression often felt by those who don't fit into heterosexual normative identity, the term quickly gained wider popularity, to an extent that Teresa de Lauretis ceased using it as she felt it had been absorbed by the very institutions she had been criticizing when she first introduced the concept. As a slang term, it denoted the oddness of being different from the norm, the strangeness of not behaving as culturally expected, anything that delegitimizes the power of domination. Queer theory has evolved into three major fields of study, all adopting the exclusion and oppression of alternative psychosexual expression as a foundational insight.

First, queer theory critiques all literature and human discourse that seeks to stabilize and make normative certain behaviors and norms to which all people are expected to subscribe. It seeks to embrace and include that which is different, unusual, strange, and at odds with popular expectation. Second, it studies the sociological and political fallout, when people and groups deviate from the prevailing norms, seeking to highlight the positive and constructive contribution of such unconventionality to the development and evolution of life. Third, there are religious implications, pertaining to the present work, seeking to highlight the alternative consciousness of prophetic and mystical movements, undermining the monopoly and domination often evoked in the name of formal religion. In a word, queer theory targets what we tend to exclude, inviting us to reexamine our motives, alerting us to subverted wisdom that perhaps should be embraced rather than subverted.

In the Christian Gospels, the parables of Jesus provide generic examples of queer theory as explained in C. H. Dodd's (1978) configuration of orientation, disorientation, and reorientation. The parable scrambles the normative structures and values, leaving the hearers baffled and confused, and unsure what to do next. The reorientation cannot be a return to the status quo (the orientation), as it no longer carries enduring credibility. The miracles—as parables in action—can be read in a similar manner. Queer theory is a serious field of study although often employing wit, sarcasm, and irony. Rather than confront powerholders with rational discourse, it seeks to make light of their seriousness and ridicules their tenacious grip on power and authority.

Luke's Exclusive Agenda

Luke is the author of the Acts of the Apostles, a book commonly regarded as Part 2 of his earlier Gospel. The entire book of Acts unfolds around one outstanding character, namely, Paul. This is Luke's great hero, often described with heroic deeds and achievements that are not congruent with Paul's own authentic letters. Luke bends history to suit his own wish to exalt his chosen hero. The queer theorist seeks to expose Luke's foundational addiction to patriarchal power, highlighting how Luke seems quite blinkered in terms of the power dynamics he often employs.

Luke wants to make sure that Paul is seen to be in full accord with authentic apostolic criteria. Paul must be seen to be in the apostolic line of succession. Consequently, Peter is brought into the story particularly in its incipient moments. And while Pater and Paul will diverge on their missionary understandings, Peter still remains a significant complement to all that Paul represents as an apostle of the authentic Gospel.

Is it also possible that Luke goes to greater lengths to establish the apostolic credibility of his hero by ensuring that his narrative is constructed on the solid foundation not only of Peter, but of the entire group of twelve? Acts 2:1–4 describes the ritual of what is commonly regarded as the first Pentecost, but the text also seems to serve a more subtle, queer purpose, namely, that of reconvoking the twelve for Luke's own endorsement of Paul's apostolic heroism. Paul must be seen to belong fully to the apostolic tradition, and Luke establishes the foundation in the original Pentecost event.

This brings us to the most critical question of all: How does Luke know that all the twelve returned for Pentecost? We know that none of the twelve were on Calvary—they all had fled in fear, disappointment, disillusionment. In Christian lore, it is widely assumed that they did come back, but we only have Luke's word for that. If they did return, how come we never again hear anything about them, apart from the references to Peter and James in the book of Acts? (The James in question tends to be regarded as the brother of Jesus and not the son of Zebedee referred to in the Gospels.)

Controversial and heretical though it may sound, I want to suggest that in all probability the entire group known as the twelve did *not* return, that the Pentecost story is effectively a Lukan invention, and that the narrative of Pentecost is a patriarchal ploy to lay solid foundations for Luke's two great heroes, Peter and Paul (particularly the latter). Inspired by the wisdom of queer theory, I want to work with those assumptions to highlight one of the most blatant structures of exclusion in the New Testament, one that has had a highly destructive impact down through the Christian centuries.

If the Pentecost story is largely a Lukan invention, where did Luke get the idea from? There are some noteworthy precedents in the Hebrew Scriptures and other ancient literary sources. The story of Pentecost strongly resembles the Old Testament Feast of the New Grain (Harvest), associated with Moses receiving the law on Mt. Senai, fifty days after the exodus from Egypt. According to legend, God issued the law in all seventy languages of humankind. Philo claimed that when the law was initially given, fire streamed from heaven, and a voice from the flame became articulate speech. The Qumran community celebrated three Pentecost feasts: the Feast of New Grain, the Feast of New Wine, and the Feast of New Oil. In Acts 2:13, the onlookers make fun: "These people are drunk." Is there some type of conflation here between the celebration of the Feast of New Grain and that of the Feast of New Wine?

The Spirit of Pentecost

There are other serious questions requiring discerning attention, most notably, what is Luke's understanding of the Holy Spirit? According to Acts 2:1–4, the Spirit is a divine life force, some kind of mystical organism, capable of reinvigorating select human beings (all male) so that they become more effective in preaching and teaching the Gospel of Jesus. The Spirit seems to be supporting and affirming the patriarchal bias that dominated the evolution of the early church. This might be regarded as an exclusive view, significantly different from the second part of Chapter 2 (Acts 2:5–11) where inclusiveness comes to the fore.

We have no way of ascertaining how Luke understood the second section of the Pentecost reading, other than highlighting these diverse visitors as being at one in their admiration for the twelve preachers. But there is a great deal more than admiration going on in this scenario. As indicated above, these diverse peoples, allegedly not yet evangelized, seem to be endowed with some remarkable gifts for discernment, gifts that all the great religions deem to be uniquely of God's own Spirit.

Our need to include—and even affirm—this latter queer group is succinctly captivated by theologian, Wendy Farley, in a book passionately desiring a church where all outsiders are embraced anew. She writes, "Christianity moves through history carried by the impulses of domination and exclusion. It despises uppity women, no-hellers, contemplatives, queers, and thinks even less of those people outside Christianity altogether. But without their witness to the nearness and tender mercies of Emmanuel, the memory of Christ is impossibly distorted" (Farley 2011, 6).

A more responsible Christian interpretation requires us to consider that these queer people of Acts 2:5–11 are already filled with the Holy Spirit. Why? Because as indicated by Genesis 1:1, the whole creation is replete with the empowering creativity of the Holy Spirit. Every creature in that same creation, human and nonhuman alike, is already blessed with the fullness of God's Spirit. The primacy of the Spirit, therefore, belongs to the second group rather than the first. The true witness to Holy Spirit is with the second rather than with the first group.

What, therefore, is the significance of the first group? Are we not witnessing a fresh injection of spiritual empowerment for the group that was so disillusioned and disoriented after the untimely death of Jesus that they need a fresh bestowal of spiritual renewal?

This resolution to our dilemma overcomes two difficulties:

1. It honors the fact that the living Spirit of God is fully at work throughout creation from the dawn of time—in the challenging words of Australian theologian, Denis Edwards (2004, 1), the Holy Spirit has been operational since the big bang and therefore is not given merely for the first time at the Christian Pentecost.
2. Those who truly believe in the power of the Holy Spirit in the description of Acts 2, comprise the second group (Acts 2:5–11) and not the first, for whom a special gifting of the Spirit is provided to lift them out of their lethargy and disbelief.

Luke's theology of the Holy Spirit fits well with the popular church's teaching of a descending patriarchal Trinity, attributing a vague and ill-defined role to the third "person." Luke lacks all sense of the exuberance of the indigenous notion of the *Great Spirit*, known across several millennia in cultures, ancient and modern alike—a subject I explore in another work (O'Murchu 2012).

Luke's Disturbing Misogyny

Now we come to the queerest twist of all in Luke's Pentecost story. Luke has been reputed for citing the examples of women more often than any other evangelist. The nineteenth-century commentator Alfred Plummer, called Luke's Gospel the "Gospel of Womanhood." In the synoptic Gospels (Matthew, Mark, and Luke), there are only two stories involving women that Luke does not record—the incident with the Syrophonecian woman and Mary's anointing of Jesus. Luke shares a few other such accounts with one or more of the other synoptic Gospels. However, Luke also records a surprising number of significant passages involving women that are unique to his Gospel, either in their entirety or in their extended female focus.

It has also been noted, however, that his regard for women is far from wholesome, employing some patriarchal biases that undermine a just and liberating dynamic. Full discipleship in Luke involves the power and authority to exorcise, heal, and preach (see Luke 9:1–6, 10:1–16). Like the other Gospel writers, Luke does not have any call narrative in which Jesus invites a woman to follow him, no women are commissioned as apostles, and none are named as disciples, although we must ask whether Luke 10:1–16 might have involved women. Instead women are healed or exorcised, and then they serve (*diakonia*). Luke shows only men empowered to speak and bear responsibility (e.g., Luke 24:33, 47–49). Women respond with silence.

Summarizing this negative picture, Jane Schaberg (1992, 275) adds,

> The Gospel of Luke is an extremely dangerous text, perhaps the most dangerous in the Bible. . . . Even as this

Gospel highlights women as included among the followers of Jesus, subjects of his teaching and objects of his
healing, it deftly portrays them as models of subordinate
service, excluded from the power center of the movement
and from significant responsibilities. Claiming the authority of Jesus, this portrayal is an attempt to legitimate male
dominance in the Christianity of the author's time.

Far from being inclusive of women's worth and apostolic
value, Luke ends up endorsing one of the worst examples of
exclusion in the entire New Testament. Luke probably knows
the full story. He knows who received the first Resurrection
commission to go forth to proclaim, and presumably he also
knows that all the twelve did not return after the disturbing
dislocation of the death of Jesus. He can't come to terms with
all that—*the fact that the first authentic Christian disciples
consisted of Mary Magdalene and her followers*! And amid his
preoccupation with his two great heroes—Peter and Paul—he
decides to bring back the twelve, thus totally eliminating the
original Resurrection witnesses, namely, Mary Magdalene and
her colleagues. Having made them invisible, his guilt rises up
to haunt him, and so he tries to reclaim some peace of mind
by inserting a token woman into the picture, namely, Mary, the
mother of Jesus. His inclusion of Mary, the Mother of Jesus,
with the twelve in the Pentecost scene betrays a disturbing level
of misogyny. He chooses a safe devotional example, a patronizing motherly figure, instead of the courageous pioneering Christian leader, Mary Magdalene.

The Pentecost story is riddled with oppressive exclusion.
Even the Spirit who breathes life into dead bones is locked into
a patriarchal masquerade. Let's reclaim the subverted women
apostles; let's honor them with a poetic epitaph as they await a
Resurrection dawn. And let's hope and pray that Christianity will
face that empty tomb sooner rather than later.

Women in Post-Resurrection Space

It was a grey dawn, and heavy spirits lingered
as the women fingered,
the spices to prepare.
While the darkness further shattered their grieving hearts
    in pain.
And there was no broken body,
their lamenting to regain.
From the hallow empty spaces, the apostles fled in fear,
leaving echoes ever haunting,
and prospects all too daunting
for the women left retrieving what scant hope there did
    remain.

The women remembered his words, mid echoes ever fading,
yet hope enough invading
for lamenting to endure.
Connecting with the apostles proved futile to the core.
They ridiculed the women,
as they often did before.
So alone they ventured out from the garden of their grief.
The Galilean mission
became their new commission.
And light began to pierce the dark mid lamenting liberty.

The fifty days of legend till Pentecost came through,
an exaggerated cue
to reclaim the scattered males.
The sacred number, fifty, denotes extended time,
as women weave the future
and adopt another rhyme.
They co-create community a-birthing for the church.
They are the first disciples

with faith that energizes.
Yet, brutally deleted from history's sacred lore.

The Pentecostal moment, an inflated Lukan tale,
cos the women did not fail
in the mission they embraced.
The church's true foundation is the women's legacy,
awaiting men's return,
the women sowed new seed.
And the infant church it sprouted, with women to the fore.
The Pauline early mission,
with women in commission.
We glimpse the truth subverted which time will yet redeem.

The truthfulness mid Spirit-power
one day will know its truth-filled hour.
And a truth too long subverted
will again be resurrected.
And lament will carve another song:
On how females do empower!

Thus we confront Pentecost with its very dark shadow—
of misogyny, oppression, and exclusion. Luke must surely have
known of the significant role of women in the early Pauline communities, the discipleship of equals that Elizabeth Schussler Fiorenza and others have highlighted. His preoccupation with his
male heroes blinkers and blinds his vision, and what ensues is
not only a disturbing example of female oppression and exclusion but probably a distorted understanding of Pentecost itself.

If we prioritize Acts 2:5–11, then indeed we see the archetypal and enduring value of Pentecost as an *recurring experience*
rather than merely a *once-off event*. The experience never ceases.
It exists eternally: "I was there when he created the world" (Prov.
8:27), or in St. Paul's words, "The Spirit searches everything, even

the depths of God"(1 Cor. 2:10). That archetypal enduring experience is what we witness in Acts 2:5–11, the Spirit who blows where she wills and can never be sequestered to any exclusive group, twelve apostles, or any other. The event of Pentecost should not be taken literally. The experience of Pentecost transcends all literary descriptions and belongs to the universal web of life itself, with the Spirit's creative explosion at the dawn of creation itself.

The Spirit Who Blows

Nothing can be excluded from the Spirit's embrace. The entire creation—from its cosmic grandeur to minute subatomic particles—must be included. That which energizes the energy, which engenders and sustains everything in creation, is nothing less than that life force we call the Holy Spirit. In our human story its most ancient naming is that of the Great Spirit, long believed to be the divine embodied empowerment of everything in creation. From this vivifying and sustaining influence of Spirit-power, nothing—and nobody—is ever excluded.

In a previous work (O'Murchu 2012), I outline the cultural and spiritual fascination, named across several contemporary indigenous cultures as the *Great Spirit*. This ancient belief considers the Spirit to be the original intuition of human belief in the mystery and influence of God. And the influence is mediated first and foremost through creation itself, more specifically through the energy force that animates and sustains everything in creation. According to this understanding, God as living Spirit comes first, the original and primordial revelation of Holy Mystery at work in creation. It is in the power of this originating Spirit that the birthing energy of creation is awakened and sustained. That which comes first in our conventional understanding of the Trinity—the Father—is also understood to be subject to the energetic influence of the Great Spirit. Similarly, with Jesus, who in traditional theology is understood as a prerequisite for the coming of the Holy Spirit, in the tradition of the Great Spirit is himself begotten of the Spirit, and—to paraphrase St. Paul—is raised to new life in the power of the Spirit.

These controversial ideas have not yet been embraced by mainline theologians. They belong to the realm of spirituality rather than formal religion. I allude to them in the present work as I detect a strong inclusive potential for the spiritual awakening that characterizes the twenty-first century. This awakening has several articulations extensively reviewed by Johnson and Ord (2012). However, Johnson and Ord give scant attention to what may be the most empowering breakthrough of all, namely, the rise of Pentecostalism in our time.

Pentecostalism—and the vast range of Pentecostal churches—is one of the most rapidly growing Christian phenomena of the twentieth and twenty-first centuries. It is generally perceived as rigidly fundamentalist, esoteric (speaking in tongues, etc.), sectarian, and scripturally superficial (prioritizing the Holy Spirit). It also tends to exhibit an exclusive self-righteousness, not only in terms of other world religions, but in relation to other Christian denominations. On closer examination, Pentecostalism exhibits another set of values, congruent with the inclusivity being explored in the present work, and these are enumerated by a widely respected Pentecostal scholar, Amos Yong:

> Pentecostal churches function as alternative social and economic networks, with congregations providing local apprenticeship systems for members, . . . Members are initiated into training programs, focused on "developing self-esteem, arming them with skills applicable to the larger social system." Some are enrolled in substance abuse programs, and inserted into rehabilitation processes, others are provided with basic financial education, and all find themselves as members of a new community. (Yong 2010, 24)

I view the rise of Pentecostalism primarily from a sociological and cultural perspective. The extensive appeal of this movement cannot be located simply in the gullibility and fundamentalist convictions of its adherents—a criticism often made by outsiders. To the contrary, we may well be witnessing a development that contributes forthrightly and proactively to the emerging global Christianity of the twenty-first century—a conviction elegantly defended by Pentecostal scholar Wolfgang Vondey (2010, 1, 5):

> The chief question in the twenty-first century is not *whether* Christian theology can be global, but *what* that global theology will look like. . . . Pentecostalism as a worldwide phenomenon unifies the theological enterprise and allows it to speak to the particularities of diverse contexts. . . . I suggest that classical Pentecostalism is a particular manifestation of the contemporary crisis in theology and responsible for bringing about the turn of Christianity toward a global agenda.

Vondey employs the metaphor of play to name and explain what makes Pentecostalism so attractive to people at the margins and so persuasive for those seeking a more vibrant and communal articulation of faith. Contrary to the staid, legalistic, and dogmatic content of so much formal Christianity, Pentecostalism has evolved into a more pliable, playful adoption of creative and imaginative expression of the Spirit who blows where she wills (without denying the deviations that sometimes ensue). "Pentecostalism," declares Vondey (2012, 44), "presents itself as a community joined together by a shared vision and imagination, a multiplicity of voices and languages that nonetheless plays together for the enjoyment of God."

If we can envisage a collaborative endeavor between faith in the Great Spirit (as articulated through first nations peoples around the world) and the aspirations of Pentecostal Christians

(as evidenced in the extensive growth of the Pentecostal movement), not only have we an exciting possibility for a new global
spirituality, but a planetary force for inclusivity far beyond the
prospects and promises of formal religions. Australian theologian, Gideon Goosen (2011) explores the inclusivity in terms
of hyphenated Christianity, describing the contemporary move
toward multiple religious belonging, and attributing this development not to some New Age syncretism but to another new
inspiration of the Spirit who blows where she wills (Goosen
2011, 128ff.). To many, it will sound like a queer combination, a
synthesis that undermines any semblance of authentic religious
belief. Might it be a prophetic articulation for how the Spirit
seeks unity for empowerment (not for conformity) in the world
of the twenty-first century, a world running far ahead of churches
and formal religions still clinging desperately to an outdated
exclusivity doomed to eventual extinction!

Chapter 12

Why Did Paul Favor the Gentiles?

The programmatic mission to the Gentiles during the course of this present world was a wrenching departure for the early church and caused so much controversy in the first Christian generation. Neither the actions nor the words of the historical Jesus had given precise and detailed instructions for such an initiative.

— JOHN P. MEIER

Christians seeking more inclusive ways of being, for themselves and for others, often begin by highlighting the inclusion of Gentiles as a primary example of Gospel-based inclusivity. While Peter and James seem to have favored the Jews, viewing Jesus as a Jewish reformer rather than the founder of a new religion, Paul embraced those seeking spiritual meaning, but not necessarily based on the Jewish faith. These varying outsiders were known as the Gentiles, sometimes called pagans. Paul's embrace of this group, and his apparent persuasion that the church in Jerusalem should accept them, marked not only the launch of the Christian faith, but also a precedent for a new inclusivity that seems to have been quite radical for its time.

For much of its history, Christian evangelization has been based on the view that since the Jews rejected Jesus as Messiah, then those promoting the message of Jesus turned to the Gentiles (pagans) from whom they received welcome and acceptance. Indeed such sentiments can be found in the Gospels themselves, particularly in John's Gospel where the "Jews" are consistently portrayed as opposing the message of Jesus.[1] Turning to the Gentiles, however, is a vision belonging to Paul rather than to Jesus, and in both cases, we are dealing with a very complex development, the intricacies of which are comprehensively reviewed by the Finnish scholar Juho Sankamo (2012).

According to Joachim Jeremias (1958), Jesus did not intend that he himself, or his disciples, would practice a Gentile mission; however, Jeremias contended, Jesus did anticipate the eventual gathering together of all God's people on Mount Zion (later identified with the Kingdom of God). In theological terms, this envisaged gathering became the basis for the ultimate coming together of all God's people in fidelity to the one God of Judaism, a vision often described as that of eschatological restoration. While it sounds very inclusive, it is actually more about imperial conformity than liberating community.

Eschatological Restoration

The eschatological gathering in of the nations, which still exerts huge appeal for fundamentalist Christians, is quite a complex subject. It is closely related to the notion of the Chosen People we met in Chapter 1 and also to the notion of monotheism already reviewed briefly in the opening chapter. We recall that the rise of *monotheistic religion* is usually attributed to the Egyptian pharaoh Akhenaton in the fourteenth century BCE. Popularly understood, monotheism proclaims the oneness of God over against the proliferation and diversity of what came to be denounced as false idols (adopted by the pagans). Overtly, the emphasis is on *unity*, embodied in one supernatural being, but covertly the issue of *power* looms large and has rarely been subjected to scholarly analysis. For some five thousand years before the time of Jesus, the ruling Sky God was envisaged and worshipped as a king, who, like earthly royal figureheads, was perceived to be endowed with unilateral supreme power. On earth that divine power was invested in, and mediated through, the king, whose power was also unquestioned and without rival.

Thus the sole divine representative on earth (i.e., the king) embodied the One God who ruled from beyond. The Jewish religion first developed the monotheistic ideology. Jewish scholars Shinan and Zakovitch (2012, 1) describe the Jewish Bible as the manifesto of the monotheistic revolution. Later, Christianity and Islam fully embraced the new outlook.

Keeping in mind this royal monotheistic influence, we can unravel the intricacies of *restoration eschatology*. For at least one thousand years before the time of Jesus, Palestine (sometimes described as Israel) endured sustained political and military interference. The people speculated on why God had betrayed them and beseeched the imperial God to rescue them from the forces of oppression. The rescuer, considered to be divinely sent, was the great King David who reigned from about BCE 1010–970. Reputedly, David achieved one military or diplomatic triumph after another against all of Israel's neighbors. This allowed him to found a small empire where Jews were relatively secure—no small feat, given the fact that Palestine was situated on a bridge between Africa, Asia, and Europe. David and his son Solomon, who succeeded him, made Israel a powerful empire for the first and last time.

For the Jewish people, the patriarch, David, exemplified such divine authority (despite some noted moral transgressions) and the hoped-for deliverer from the oppressive forces. The "Son of David" became an emblematic figure for the awaited Messiah, who would deliver a final sense of freedom in which all the people would be gathered as one and enjoy the restored love and protection of God. Allegedly, this utopian ideal sustained the people of Israel for several subsequent centuries, and orthodox Jews still await this final deliverer. Although Christians claim that the final deliverance was achieved in the historical person of Jesus, they too still wait for the end-of-the-age breakthrough, the subject of much wild speculation over the past two thousand years.

Today, both Jews and Christians subscribe to the notion of *eschatological restoration*. This is the broad outline: in time God will restore the kingship of David, reestablishing Israel as God's Chosen People. And this time round, something dramatic will take place—metaphorically described as an ingathering of all the nations around the holy mountain in Jerusalem (Mt. Zion)—in which all people on earth will be gathered in submission to God—through God's primary representative on earth, King David's successor.

Both Jews and Christians regard this utopian restoration as revealed truth, which many believers interpret in a literal fashion. However, for more informed contemporary readers (listeners), much of this material sounds fanciful and far-fetched. It is popular mythology created around a number of historical allusions. Despite this questionable background, we must acknowledge how crucially important it has been, and still remains, for biblical scholarship and for mainline Christian theology. It is also hugely significant for a sector of Judeo-Christian scholarship, which claims that Jesus fully, or substantially, endorsed such eschatological restoration, situating Jesus as a reformer of Judaism rather than the founder of a new Gentile-based religion.[2]

Jesus and the Gentiles

According to the Finnish scholar Juho Sankamo (2012, 281), Jesus did not explicitly command the disciples to proclaim the Gospel to the Gentiles; nor did he himself travel or participate in any formal mission to Gentile peoples. The early Christians (including the apostles) considered the Resurrection of Jesus to be proof that the eschatological time had arrived. In the light of the Jewish aspirations of eschatological consummation and Israel's restoration, Jesus' Jewish disciples might have reasoned that the Gospel was to be preached to the Gentiles because the eschatological time had arrived. In the context of the Jewish eschatological vision, the salvation of the Gentiles belonged to the era of the "eschaton," that ultimate consummation that would fulfil the hopes long invested in the "Son of David." According to this understanding, Jesus might have (probably did) include the Gentiles, because the new eschatological breakthrough being inaugurated in and through Jesus would have embraced everybody, irrespective of creed or nationality.

The eschatological hour had arrived—the deliverance made possible through the death and Resurrection of Jesus—suggesting that the gathering of all nations on Mt. Zion was already taking place. That in-gathering would include everybody, not only the Jews. However, in the judgment that would follow, the Jews would gain favorable divine approval above and beyond all other peoples.

In the closing decades of the twentieth century, several scholars, Jewish and Christian, addressed this issue. Geza Vermes and E. P. Sanders are two oft-quoted advocates, viewing the mission to the Gentiles as one of *incorporation into the eschatological coming together of all God's people and not as a separate entity that in time came to be seen as the foundation of a new and different religion, namely, Christianity.* Thus writes E. P. Sanders (1985, 212), "One of the surest proofs that Jesus' career is to be seen within the general context of Jewish eschatological expectations is that the movement which he initiated spawned a Gentile mission."

However, we now know that the eschatological expectation is more of a utopian aspiration than a historical or religious fact in any sense. It appears that Jesus did make contact with Gentiles, and encouraged his followers to do the same. In fact, some scholars suggest that the inclusive mission of the Gentiles begins with Jesus rather than with Paul. It seems that Jesus dealt directly with a number of people identified as Gentiles (pagans), notably the Syrophoenician woman (Mark 7:24–30; Matt. 15:21–28), the centurion (Matt. 8:5–10; Luke 7:1–10), the Gerasene demoniac (Mark 5:1–20; Matt. 8:28–34; Luke 8:26–39). Were these exceptional or chance happenings in the ministry of the historical Jesus, or might they serve as indicators of a more extensive mission of Jesus among Gentile peoples, which would also help to explain Jesus' travels in or near areas inhabited largely by Gentiles (e.g., Deacapolis, Tyre, Sidon)? Scholars also detect implicit allusions to the Gentiles in texts, such as Gentiles dining in the company of Abraham (Matt. 8:11–12; Luke 13:28–29), Matthew's reference to Galilee of the Gentiles (Matt. 4:13, 15), Luke's apparent wish to have Jesus befriend the Samaritans (Luke 10:25–37, 17:11–19), despite the fact that Mark and Matthew make no allusions to Jesus traveling in Samaria.[3] Many scholars also assume that the Gentiles are included in Matthew's envisioned mission to all the nations (Matt. 28:18–20).

Having thoroughly examined the complexities of this issue, Juho Sankamo (2012), opines that the historical Jesus made a clear preferential option for mission among the Jewish peoples. Consequently, Jesus did not *consciously* include the Gentiles, but because he embraced and endorsed the belief in an eschatological restoration, he unambiguously envisaged the Gentiles being included in that final in-gathering.

The modern reader can hardly be blamed for concluding that Jesus was embracing the Gentiles begrudgingly rather than openly. One begins to wonder if the historical Jesus has not been ensnared in the ideological and mythological agendas of the time, and if scholars, ancient and modern, are not also deluded by ancient imperial concerns. Did Jesus himself become ensnared in such agendas? Or was it the evangelists, conditioned by their time and culture, that end up depicting Jesus as a Jewish patriarchal ideologue rather than a messianic liberator embracing a larger worldview?

Scholars such as Abel M. Bibliowicz (2013), maintain that the rejection of Judaism in much Christian tradition arises from a protracted and bitter struggle about identity, legitimacy, and authority during the early decades of the second century, and continued well into the fifth century. Tensions between Jews and "Christians" probably first arose after the Roman invasion (66–70 CE), when the Jewish people had to redefine their identity without the temple, which was now destroyed. From here on, Christians began to evolve along increasingly separate lines, although their bedrock tradition initially was that of Judaism.

Paul and the Gentiles

When it comes to St. Paul, we seem to be into much clearer territory. However, Paul's mission to the Gentiles is also a subject of intense research, with no shortage of controversy and sometimes bitterly disputed adversarial positions. Eung Chun Park (2003, 2), notes that Paul did distinguish between a Torah-bound Gospel, addressed in the letter to the Galatians, with a central emphasis on circumcision, and a Torah-free Gospel, explored in the letters to the Romans and to the Philippians, interpreting circumcision more in terms of a spiritual disposition rather than a literal fact. According to Eung Chun Park, Paul accepted both within his view of an expanded Judaism, and was happy to retain both, accommodating the ensuing diversity that inevitably would arise. On this assessment, Paul certainly deserves to be hailed as a champion of radical inclusivity.

The critical question then is how we interpret Paul's engagement with the Gentiles—with its implications for the later evolution of Christian identity. Clearly, Paul is concerned that the inclusion and incorporation of the Gentiles—whether understood eschatologically or otherwise—should be facilitated as far as possible to enhance total acceptance. In this process, did Paul actually transgress Jewish religious (cultural) norms, or was he merely interpreting the rules in accordance with the deeper values of the Jewish law (Torah)? Again, this is a question upon which scholars do not agree, one to which we are never likely to resolve to everybody's satisfaction.

Eung Chun Park (2003, 76) pushes the inclusive horizon to a degree that is unlikely to be widely endorsed, claiming that Paul's vision is based on a theological recognition that God accepts human beings just as they are, irrespective of religious background: "That is the quintessential meaning of the grace of God as Paul understands it," an all-embracing vision best captivated in the broad spectrum of Romans 11: 33–36, inclusive of everything in God's creation, human and nonhuman alike.

What would have inspired Paul to opt for this enlarged inclusive vision? Several Jewish scholars, and those sympathetic to them, claim that such an expanded horizon is already endemic to Paul's own Jewish upbringing, particularly in the context of the eschatological in-gathering described above. Others, notably the Talmudic scholar Daniel Boyarin (1994), argue that Paul's theology of the Spirit is more deeply rooted in Hellenistic Judaism than generally believed, leading Paul toward a missionary ideal whereby all can be included in God's salvific desire.

Both Acts and Paul's letter to the Galatians describe Paul and Peter in contention concerning whether it was appropriate to proselytize among the Gentiles. Peter, the head of the Christian movement, and his followers believed that in order for Gentiles to become Christian, they must first convert to Judaism. Converted Gentiles and Jews should then continue to uphold the Torah and all the laws and rituals that Judaism entailed, including temple rituals and practices. Not everybody agrees with this juxtaposition of Paul and Peter, suggesting that their differing views are more complex than initially envisaged.

Paul, some argue, is not claiming that Peter's option for the Jew is wrong. Instead, it appears that Paul envisaged the law had already been fulfilled in and through Jesus, and consequently, it was no longer necessary to observe the laws and rituals of Judaism. It appears that Paul and Peter arrived at a compromise, where Jewish converts would continue to practice the law of Moses, while Gentile converts would not be required to so. During the Council of Jerusalem in 50 AD, it was determined that Gentiles would be accepted by all Jews into the Christianity movement and that certain Jewish practices were not necessary for their inclusion, especially circumcision.

Incorporating the Gentiles

Increasingly, scholars seem to be moving toward a consensus that Paul envisaged discipleship of Jesus as a fulfillment of Torah-based Judaism and not as an alternative to it. It seems Paul never abandoned his Jewish faith; nor did he expect converts to Jesus discipleship to do so. And in his embrace of the Gentiles, he seems to have envisaged a conversion to Judaism, without imposing all that would be required of fully fledged Jews (e.g., circumcision). Although we will never know for certain, it seems that such Jewish-Gentile integration continued to flourish up till about 70 CE.

The first Jewish-Roman war raged from 66 to 73 CE, and its destructive impact lasted well into the second century. The fate of Jewish-Christianity changed dramatically with the slaughter and deportation of Jews. Jewish Christians were largely located in and around Jerusalem. Therefore, the majority were killed or deported, essentially uprooting Christianity from among the Jewish settlements in the Palestinian region.

As Jewish Christianity dwindled into extinction by the second century, it was the Gentiles who took over the mantle of Christianity, continuing the struggle for the survival of their religion over against Roman persecution. First, Christians were seen as a sect of the Jewish religion, which was disdained in the Roman Empire, as it conflicted with the worship of the

Greco-Roman Gods. Christians and Jews were also known for their zealous revolts. Furthermore, many in the Roman Empire believed that Christianity offended the Greco-Roman Gods, which is why Paul and Peter were blamed for the Great Fire of Rome in 64 AD, allegedly leading to their martyrdom.

On the other hand, Christianity was not without some attractive elements, especially for those trapped among the lower rungs of Roman society such as peasants and slaves. As a hopelessly oppressed people in the Roman Empire, Christianity provided them with meaning to endure suffering now and thus reap the rewards in a salvation hereafter. Even many in the middle and upper classes found favor in Christianity, due to many of its altruistic teachings, along with the fact that Christian doctrine encouraged slaves to remain faithful to their masters.

However, Christians would remain a fringe religion in the Roman Empire until Christianity was legalized in the fourth century. Henceforth, it was not the break with Judaism that became critical but the radical departure from the Gospel message of empowering inclusivity. Imperial favor prioritized the strong and powerful, embracing the masses as long they remained codependently subservient to the powers of church and state. Insider/outsider status was defined along new demarcation lines that would remain in force well into the twentieth century. The inclusive aspirations of the bedrock tradition were largely abandoned, and their retrieval is an unfinished task even in the twenty-first century.

The Twenty-first Century

How do we transport the scholarly concerns on the Jewish-Gentile relationship into the context of the twenty-first century? And how do we employ the ongoing debate so that it serves a new inclusivity rather than continue to perpetuate a divisive and adversarial rhetoric?

Scholars of a more Jewish persuasion claim that the foundational wisdom of Judaism, as embodied in the Torah (Jewish law) is as inclusive as one can hope to obtain in any religious system (e.g., Cook 2008; Garber 2011, Levine 2007). From this they go on to argue that the foundational integrity of Judaism should be acknowledged and fostered above and beyond any prioritizing of Christian faith (understood to have evolved from Gentile origins).

Every major world religion claims an original purity and integrity that has been undermined and diminished through translation over time. As I argue in another work (O'Murchu 2011), such erosion of deeper meaning seems to have happened in our overspiritualization of the notion of the Gospel vision of the Kingdom of God (the Companionship of Empowerment). I suspect that the foundational tenets and truths of the Torah are all to be found in the Christian vision of the new companionship. Should Christians therefore abandon the vision of the New Reign of God and simply return to Torah following? Would it not be more compelling to argue that the Torah organically evolved into the vision of the Kingdom, and therefore the latter is the more appropriate for both Christians and Jews to embrace today?

For the twenty-first century, we also need to discern a way forward acknowledging growing evidence for religious pluralism and *multiple religious belonging* (cf. Gideon Goosen 2011, 27ff.). In the eyes of many religionists, such pluralism is viewed as a new brand of Gentile paganism. Increasingly people of adult faith realize that commonalities are more important than differences. Historically, Christianity evolved out of Judaism as a contemporary world religion, amid diverse and pluralistic cultures, Christianity itself must evolve into a richer complexity open to learning from the wisdom not only of Judaism, but of all the other faith systems and other spiritual movements that transcend all formal religions (cf. Johnson and Ord 2012). Not only is this an evolutionary desirable thing to do, but as indicated throughout this book, there are many Gospel prerogatives for such cultural and religious inclusivity.

Chapter 13

Constantine's Disastrous Triumphalism

By Constantine's gift, Christianity was both officially established and fatally compromised.

— Barbara Tuchman

From an energetic movement of faith, [the church] coagulated into a phalanx of required beliefs, thereby laying the foundation for every succeeding Christian fundamentalism for centuries to come.

— Harvey Cox

Christianity's climb to dominance was sparked by a single event—the conversion of Roman Emperor Constantine I. Constantine was involved in a bitter civil war to retain the emperor's throne. Before the decisive clash with Maxentius, his brother-in-law and chief rival in 312 CE, it is claimed that he experienced a vision where Christ appeared to him, instructing him to place the sign of Christ on the banners carried by his troops. He did so, and his army proceeded to demolish that of his rival, securing his position as emperor. He credited the Christian God for his resounding victory and proceeded to favor Christianity over all other religions throughout his massive empire.

Almost overnight, Christianity was propelled to the status of a global, theological powerhouse. In the words of Wendy Farley (2011, 189), "When Constantine gained his military victory under the sign of the Cross, the conflation of the Kingdom of God and the Empire of Caesar became an essential part of Christian history and theology." In the space of just one century—the fourth of the Christian era—fourteen church councils were convened, nearly all at the behest of the emperor. Roman citizens and subjects converted in droves, as Christians were afforded special tax breaks and other amenities not available to any other religious affiliations.

In fact, all other religions were outlawed by Constantine. It would not be until later in the fourth century (380 CE), that Christianity was declared to be the official state religion of Rome, making illegal all other models of worship. This would ensure the conversion of nearly everyone under Roman control, covering much of Europe, West Asia, and North Africa. Failing to convert could ensue in deportation or execution.

Constantine favored Christianity for one main reason: it could/would be a powerful force for unity throughout the empire. His goal was inclusivity but envisaged for reasons far from noble and very much at variance with the Jesus he proclaimed to be *Pantocrator* (Ruler of the Universe). Constantine's religious aspiration was *conformity, control, and domination.* The Christian religion was the tool that would reinforce his unilateral power, a very different aspiration from the Gospel's Companionship of Empowerment.

Conformity and Exclusivity

In addition to promoting Christianity within the world's largest empire at the time, Constantine also forced various Christian leaders to unify the diverse doctrines that had evolved since the inception of Christianity. Today, we tend to assume that Christians are—and were—united around the understanding of faith outlined in the four Gospels. Firstly, the four were only named (by St. Iraneus) around 180–85 CE. It would be almost another one hundred years before the Canon of Scripture would evolve. As Bart Ehrman (2011) vividly illustrates, those early Christian centuries were characterized by great diversity of thought and religious views, and often among Christians themselves fiercely heated debates and disagreements prevailed.

Constantine imposed conformity, not only for social or political reasons, but also to restrain the divergent differences that often accompanied the maturing of the Christian faith, a sense of divergence that can be traced back to the New Testament period itself (cf. Dunn 1990). Unfortunately this desire to control also seriously curbed any semblance of religious freedom within the embryonic movement; it succeeded in centralizing the power structure of the church, strengthening its influence, and laying a power base upon which Christianity would grow and flourish for several subsequent centuries! But as we shall see presently, it was a flourish sustained by the patriarchal will to power rather than the Gospel blueprint for empowering liberation.

The First Council of Nicaea (in modern Turkey) was called by Constantine in 325 CE, with the purpose of resolving these common doctrinal controversies. The primary point of contention of the day concerned the nature of Jesus Christ. Arianism argued that Jesus was created by the father (therefore a separate being), while orthodoxy contended that the Father and the Son were of the same substance. The resolution adopted to combat Arianism is the Nicene Creed. In the continuing controversy, Athanasius was the chief advocate of orthodoxy, and because of his labors the orthodox position prevailed. The Council of Constantinople in 381 CE essentially ended the controversy by reaffirming the condemnation of Arianism.

While the most pressing doctrinal controversy was rectified in Nicaea, there were still a large number of Christian texts floating around, many of which contradicted one another. In order to bring an end to the confusion, church leaders commenced the Council of Rome in 382 CE to determine which books should be canonized and included in the authorized scriptural collection (later known as the Bible). A variety of factors were considered in selecting texts, including doctrinal congruency and authenticity. Other more arbitrary factors also came into play. For instance, it was determined that four gospel texts had to be included, no more or no less, to represent the "four corners" of the earth.

Even though doctrinal inconsistencies had been resolved, there was not yet an established hierarchy within the Christian church. In 451 CE, the Council of Chalcedon was convened to establish a defined hierarchy, or a centrally operated Christian church. Christianity had traditionally been stronger in the East, in bishoprics such as Antioch, Alexandria, Jerusalem, and Constantinople. But the church headquarters was awarded to the bishopric of Rome, with the bishopric of Constantinople recognized as second in power.

It was generally understood that Peter, the head of Christendom upon the death of Christ, was the original bishop of Rome. Therefore, it stood to reason that the Roman bishops represented the true apostolic succession for the entire Christian movement. In addition, Rome was the epicenter of the Roman Empire, so basing the Christian church in Rome enabled close coordination of political and ecclesiastic leadership. With this decision, the loosely organized and decentralized "Christian church" became the highly centralized Roman Catholic Church.

Early Christianity seems to have been characterized by a great deal of diversity, and it appears that St. Paul approvingly supported such diversity by creating ecclesial groups characterized by fluidity and flexibility. This rich diversity was gradually depleted as the urge to create an imposing conformity gained momentum, particularly in the fourth century, as indicated above. The ideological distinction between insiders and outsiders was not as strong in the bedrock tradition as in subsequent centuries. There were certainly norms and expectations, but couched in a sense of welcome and shared hospitality. The Gospel norm of radical inclusiveness had already been diluted by the Gospel writers themselves; nonetheless that inclusive spirit continued to inspire and animate Christian fellowship up to, and in some cases beyond, the monopolizing conformity of Constantine in the fourth century.

The Birth of Clericalism

Upon the collapse of the Western Roman Empire in 476 CE, secular authority broke down throughout the former imperial lands. As invading Germanic tribes took control of former territory, the rule of law became virtually nonexistent. The Christian (Catholic) church was one of the few organizations that could offer some semblance of law and order, ensuing in the masses looking to the church first and foremost for guidance during this chaotic time. Thus the power and influence of the church continued to grow. Church governance became synonymous with social and political order, and progressively morphed into a new elite heavily committed to the distinction between insiders and outsiders.

Gradually the clergy emerged as the group with unprecedented access to patriarchal power. The clergy were typically among the few who became literate and educated. All knowledge came under the influence of the prevailing religious wisdom, which viewed the masses as passive recipients in need of the wherewithal that would procure salvation in a life hereafter. The clergy saw themselves as God's primary agents to deliver truth at every level, secular and religious alike. Thus the church became a centralized patriarchal institution validated by what it considered to be an unquestioned, and unquestionable, divine mandate. The church belonged primarily to the clergy, with the people of God subverted to varying degrees of exclusion. And this understanding of the church prevailed well into the twentieth century.

The clerical monopoly was facilitated by a clearly defined chain of command from the pope at the top (the equivalent of the divine king), and various intermediary players between the leader at the top and the masses at the base of the pyramid. The chief intermediaries were bishops and priests, with the latter being the ones most directly impacting upon the faith of the people. All the intermediaries were male, and for much of the time, they were officially celibate, a requirement with a confusing and ambivalent history for much of Christendom.

The clericalized church quickly replaced the power of Gospel truth with the truth of imperial (divine) power. What the pope-bishop-priest declared and taught was deemed to be the revealed word of God, which the faithful refused to accept at great risk to their lives and safety. Divine power was portrayed as a power to exercise dominion and judgment. Those who rejected the power of the ruling clerics were judged to have rejected God himself—outside the church and therefore barred from heaven. And there was an unambiguous distinction between the righteous, who obeyed and remained faithful, and those who betrayed the cause and were deemed to be banished forever. The only inclusivity in this system was that of total subservience.

Papal Imperialism

Antonio Gonzalez (2012) provides a comprehensive analysis of how the egalitarian empowering vision of Jesus (the Kingdom of God) was subverted, predominantly by Constantine, and in time was substantially replaced by what came to be known as *the divine right of kings*. It resulted in a tussle for power between kings and bishops (including popes) that lasted well into the 1800s.

The Holy Roman Empire was an attempt to revive the Western Roman Empire, whose legal and political structure deteriorated during the fifth and sixth centuries, to be replaced by independent kingdoms ruled by Germanic nobles. Although the borders of the empire shifted greatly throughout its history, its principal area was always that of the German states. From the tenth century, its rulers were elected German kings, who usually sought, but did not always receive, imperial coronation by the popes in Rome.

The empire called itself "Roman" because it claimed succession to the ancient Roman Empire and "holy" because it held control over mainstream European Christianity. It was as much *political* as it was *religious*—the church *was* the state. The popes claimed leadership by saying that the empire was merely the political arm of the church, established and maintained by "God and the papacy." Under this arrangement, the emperor was answerable to the pope who could depose of the king at will—a situation that actually occurred on a number of occasions.

Kings often employed bishops in administrative affairs and frequently determined who would be appointed to ecclesiastical offices. In the wake of the Cluniac Reforms, increasingly, the papacy viewed this political involvement as inappropriate and undesirable. The reform-minded Pope Gregory VII was determined to oppose such practices, leading to the investiture controversy with the Roman Emperor Henry IV (1056–1106), who repudiated the pope's interference and persuaded his bishops to excommunicate the pope. The pope, in turn, excommunicated the king, declared him deposed, and dissolved the oaths of loyalty made to Henry. (For more information, see www.nobility-association.com/theholyromanempire.htm.)

By the time the empire eventually fell, the institutional church had become the dominant power with all the trappings of imperial might. And along the way, it had colluded with other imperial forces such as military violence, economic capitalism, and colonial subversion. In the 1920s, faced with the awakening desire for democratic modes of governance, and the consequent eclipse of imperial kingship, the Catholic Church—by instituting the feast of Christ the King—appealed to the people of Europe to hold on to kingship as God's favored political structure.

Historically, this could be seen as the church's last desperate attempt to uphold Constantine's legacy. Already Protestant theologians of the nineteenth century were seeking to reclaim the long-subverted counter-culture of the Kingdom of God (the new companionship). Not until the biblical revival after the Second World War in Europe, did Scripture scholars create a more united front, with a growing consensus that the New Testament notion of the *Kingdom of God* had been subverted over several centuries and now should be boldly and uncompromisingly reclaimed. The ensuing revolution, with its empowering and inclusive vision, is a work still in progress.

Nonimperial Egalitarianism

Today, a well-established cohort of scholars (in Scripture and theology), and a rapidly growing body of lay adult Christians, seek to retrieve and reclaim what was subverted due to Constantinian imperialism. Intellectually and intuitively, contemporary Christians are becoming highly suspicious of the sanctioned holy rhetoric about divine power and glory, and all the ecclesiastical trappings created in its name. Behind the false veneer is a deeper truth that time has not eroded and, in fact, never will. The Gospels proclaim it as a *New Reign of God*, afire with empowering liberating truth. And its inclusive embrace has a particularly strong appeal faced as we are with the fragmented, divided world of the twenty-first century.

Antonio Gonzalez (2012), a Spanish theologian of Mennonnite background, is one of several contemporary scholars pioneering the rehabilitation of Christianity's subverted truth. Jesus proclaimed the reign of God as opposed to the reign of Caesar. Within God's reign, God governs with mercy, love, justice, and special concern for the oppressed. Imbued with this faith, a new community of believers developed, particularly among the poor, who lived what Jesus proclaimed, sharing resources and practicing equality and forgiveness rather than exploitation and retribution.

Gonzalez, drawing on the research of social scientists, such as Richard Horsley, Bruce Malina, and Richard Rohrbaugh, indicates that Christianity prospered within the context of households (*oikumene*) *supported by egalitarian village subsistence. In this environment*, there was an extraordinary degree of gender and class equality. His analysis anticipates the ultimate destination of his argument for a non–state-supported, small community Christianity, and for one that does not hide the trappings of empire behind traditional claims to hierarchy. In what transpired to be the small ecclesial communities (pioneered by St. Paul), Gonzalez detects ancient models for what many people are seeking today—in church and world alike: organic, sustainable microenterprises capable of counteracting the marauding impact of corporate greed, ecological exploitation, and human degradation.

Thus the long cherished—and long subverted—vision of the Companionship of Empowerment provides enduring and sustaining hope for all who yearn for a better world, where justice, inclusivity, and empowerment can flourish for all and for the fragmented earth itself.

The Postcolonial Critique

Over the centuries, many attempts have been made to call the church to a greater sense of mutual accountability, and for most of the time, the church has responded in a defensive, imperial manner. Time and again, ecclesiastical power has been portrayed and proclaimed as divinely mandated and beyond human question and challenge. Both scholarship and spiritual discernment of the twentieth century consistently seeks to unmask and rectify the deleterious impact of such unilateral power. Of the different articulations employed by those seeking reform, I find the movement known as *postcolonialism* to be more penetrating and sustainable. And it brings into clearer relief the radical inclusivity that the present work seeks to salvage.

Postcolonialism is not about developments that happen after a period of colonization, usually described as neocolonialism. Instead it focuses on the residue of the colonial mind-set, seeking to unmask, illuminate, and confront the colonial baggage that it still clings to long after the colonizing forces have departed. Many of the Christian churches use garments for official occasions such as liturgies and other solemn occasions. Much of this garb is borrowed from, and in some cases is virtually identical to, the garments worn by the elite in ancient Roman times. Much of the paraphernalia donned by bishops in the various Christian denominations is unashamedly regal, with all the connotations of imperial power and glory.

The postcolonial critique poses a simple direct question: why do we cling to such practices with all the connotations of an imperial power so alien to the historical Jesus and to the central project of the Gospels, the New Reign of God? To which I wish to add, in the context of the present work, and why do we continue to collude with such power games when they unambiguously militate against the radical inclusivity of our bedrock faith tradition? At the root of the many oppressive exclusions that prevail in our world today (including the Christian churches) is the abuse of power. In recent years, we have been highlighting the fact that clerical sex abuse is first and foremost an abuse of power (rather than of sex); what we have not yet named or clarified is that the abuse of power involved in sexual exploitation is itself a by-product of a more invasive and pervasive corruption of power—the deeper context that postcolonialism seeks to address (more in O'Murchu 2012).

Postcolonial scholarship also highlights the several collusions we adopt—subconsciously for the greater part—in various forms of colonial mimicry in which we can all too easily become ensnared. Feminists have long denounced the patriarchal structuring of power relations and the disempowering exclusions that ensue for women particularly. Yet, in several contemporary situations, women themselves have colluded with these structures by aligning themselves with mainline politics, economics, and social organization. In good faith they attach themselves to dysfunctional systems on the belief that they can best create change from within. Unfortunately, the evidence shows that in several cases, they end up colluding with the very structures they hoped to change and thus become part of the problem rather than its resolution.

The empowerment proclaimed in the parabolic wisdom of the Gospels offers more long-term hope and promise. The colonial baggage can only be dislodged (1) by more critical awareness of oppression being endured, (2) by employing a more subversive use if imagination to conjure up alternatives, and(3) by choosing an alternative space open to the creative freedom needed to explore new ways of being and new ways of acting. Thus bell hooks (2004, 159) (who always spells her name in lower case letters), feminist poet and theologian, writes,

> I make a definite distinction between that marginality which is imposed by oppressive structures and that marginality one chooses as site of resistance—as location of radical openness and possibility. This site of resistance is continually formed in that segregated culture of opposition that is our critical response to domination. . . . We are transformed, individually, collectively, as we make radical creative space which affirms and sustains our subjectivity, which gives us new location from which to articulate our sense of the world.

Postcolonialism, offers a more informed and incisive access to what bell hooks calls the new location from which we can view our world afresh. And this, too, is what the Companionship of Empowerment entails: a freshly empowering vision, building on the past, while seeking to discard unnecessary baggage, creatively engaging the present cognizant of the untidy nature of all evolutionary growth and development, and embracing a future of greater hope and promise: a future that will seek to include and engage the diverse gifts of all creatures, animate and inanimate alike.

The election of Pope Francis, as head of the Catholic Church in March 2013 created fresh hope among Catholics that he would rein in and reform the power of the Roman Curia. As I write, Francis seems to be undertaking that task with courage and integrity. Reforming the institutions at the top, however, is not likely to achieve much without a consciousness shift on the part of Catholics universally. Catholic patriarchal triumphalism needs to be undone from the base upward and not only from the top down. And it needs to be a collective, communal endeavor—radically inclusive—in service of the Companionship of Empowerment. I hope that this book, in however small a way, will encourage all Christians to embrace, in a more courageous and proactive way, this enduring ideal of our Gospel faith.

Chapter 14

Being an Inclusive Christian Today

Why is it that so many of us do not even connect anymore in the day-to-day living out of our religion with Christ's ancient vision of inclusiveness?

— BARBARA FIAND

An inclusive church is not an expression of secular liberalism but a fundamental Gospel imperative.

— GILES FRASER

Everybody desires friendship, love, and acceptance. Everybody likes to be in, while being left outside creates feelings of alienation, pain, resentment, and distrust on a universal scale. Every religion upholds a vision of inclusivity, distinguishing between those who belong denominationally and everybody else, which they claim to hold with love and respect. Tragically, we know that is not the case amid the religious bigotry and the recurring religious violence that still endures even in the twenty-first century.

The Christian ideal, which has been explored in the present work, also embodies paradoxes and contradictions. Most Christian denominations look down on the other as being inferior to itself. Denominations rival on issues of faith and morals. Shared experiences of prayer and worship are, in fact, quite rare. Religious multiple belonging, alluded to in previous chapters, is a minority experience shared mainly by Western intellectuals. As a Christian people, we have a long way to go to realize the challenge of the Gospels to translate inclusivity into daily life.

Some Christians fear the risk of compromising ideals, in terms of the invitation to become more inclusive. They expect certain standards to be observed—ethical, cultural, devotional. Is loving one's enemies acceptable when the enemies have engaged in warfare where innocent women and children have been killed? What sexual morality are we embracing if all orientations are welcome at our Eucharistic table? Are swindlers and drunks acceptable in our midst, even when they transgress normative expectations of decency and decorum? Surely the notion of responsible boundaries also has a place in Christian behavior?

These are reasonable and common concerns. Part of our problem trying to appropriate more radical Christian values, such as Gospel inclusivity, is the lack of forums to explore the above questions in an authentically adult way. We employ the notion of dialogue quite liberally, but it is, in fact, a rare achievement either in Christian engagement or indeed in any major religious context. Capacities, such as attentive listening, informed speaking, mutual challenge, and genuine discernment, are central to responsible and creative dialogue, and the appropriate training to engage in such dialogue is not widely employed in religious organizations. Several issues arise here for the Christian person, variously related to life in the church, and a range of different ways in which people engage with church life.

Toward an Inclusive Church

At the outset, we need to acknowledge that for millions of Christians around the world, church life basically means "business as usual." Church is above all else a place to attend for Sunday worship, fulfilling an obligation to reassure the prospect of eternal life after our earthly sojourn. For such believers, inclusivity is not even an issue. To the contrary, they resent being reminded that church is a reality for all to engage with for the building of a faith community. They don't want such engagement; they see no point in becoming so involved. The key issue here is that of adult faith development to address an underdeveloped sense of faith that, over time, has become congealed and dysfunctional. Sadly, of course, these are the very people who will tend to forego opportunities for adult faith development.

The reflections of this book will have little to offer such people. Instead I am targeting people with a more developed sense of faith, adult criticality, and yearning for more engaging ways to articulate their commitment to living out the Gospel. For some, this desire initially arises from a deeper sense of involvement in local church and the growing realization that things could be different: more participative, engaging, open, and receptive to new ways of being and understanding. Increasingly, this renewed awakening comes from the people, not from their pastors, inevitably leading to disappointment, frustration, and even departure, if clergy cannot engage meaningfully. Sometimes, clergy persons experience the same disillusionment due to difficult relationships with bishops or the frustration of being unable to catalyze a more participative experience of church.

At the local church level, the awakening can take several years, with a small group of committed reformists keeping alive the dream of a deeper more inclusive vision. In some parishes, a range of new structures can unfold, including sodalities, reading groups, social action programs, parochial forums (e.g., an active parish council), right up to the creation of Basic Christian Communities, sometimes called BCCs. In this evolving context, the sense of hospitality tends to be strong, and the welcome for outsiders transparent and inspiring.

Inclusivity from beyond the Church

Various endeavors to make the church more inclusive, and conducive to inclusive ministry, continue to flourish on a universal scale. It seems, however, that the strongest driving force for such inclusivity comes from outside rather than from within the ecclesiastical realm. Several expressions have been noted:

- People who one time were closely affiliated, and drifted away for various reasons, seek reentry or a new sense of connection. This may arise for personal reasons or from some unexpected life crisis related to self or family. It may also arise from a shift of awareness around the meaning of faith in contemporary life, related to my next major category.
- People who have embarked on a spiritual search, sometimes arising from a life crisis, but more commonly today related to retirement, and a new search for meaning related to older life stages. This seems to be a more common phenomenon in the West than elsewhere and noticeably so in the United States and Canada.
- The influence of living in our information-saturated world in which people's mental and intellectual abilities are more stretched, exhibiting expanded levels of curiosity, interest, openness, receptivity, and adventure. These are people seeking insight that is intellectually congruent, not to be confused with academic learning. Again, many such people belong to the latter half of life.
- The spiritual seekers of the twenty-first century play a significant role in awakening a more generic sense of

inclusivity. This is quite an amorphous group, including some who have abandoned formal religion or outgrown the felt need for it, while also including some who did not grow up with a specific religion or spiritual practice. They tend to view formal religion in a negative light, as being archaic, irrelevant, or ensnared in religious bureaucracy. Inclusivity is a big issue for these adherents. Sometimes they are denounced and dismissed as New Agers, a castigation frequently lacking in mature discernment.

- People with a sense of social conscience, activists, justice seekers, people for whom faith is more about social action, or volunteering programs, rather than prayer or devotion. Such people can experience a painful sense of how others are oppressed and excluded, and often are acutely aware that such exclusion betrays our allegiance to the Gospels. This group also includes a small but growing body of people committed to environmental care and ecologically based justice.

- People who themselves have suffered from exclusion, for example, divorced, remarried people being told that they cannot receive Holy Communion; gay/lesbian people not feeling welcomed in a church gathering; people acquainted with the pain and trauma of clerical sex abuse. Through the experience of being excluded, they have become advocates for inclusivity and often embark upon reading and study on the evidence for the Gospel inclusivity described in the present work.

Revisiting the Gospels

Finally, the desire for a greater sense of inclusivity comes from a range of Christians revisiting, studying, and praying the Gospels. No longer can the wisdom of sacred text be reserved to the church's teaching authority, on the one hand, or to academic scholars, on the other. In a strangely unexpected way, the one-time notion of the *sensus fidelium* (the sense of the faithful) is coming back to haunt us and challenge us afresh. People read more, avail themselves of educational opportunities for adult faith formation, seek out information on the Internet, and join study or discussion groups.

Some go a step further and create a reading group or begin to avail themselves of workshops and conferences attended merely by specialists just a few years ago. They invite their friends, thus casting wider the net of inclusivity.

Thus there is arising, particularly in the West, a new religious (many would prefer the word: *spiritual*) avant-garde, some critical of formal religion, others simply dismissive of it. And still others, as indicated above, who do want to bring their newly discovered wisdom back into the church. That reintegration tends not to be an easy process; often the clergy themselves have not kept up with the reading, study, and reflection, and therefore feel threatened by those embracing the new wisdom. And the negative—or indifferent—response from the clergy is what subsequently can lead to new forms of exclusion and possibly a sense of rejection.

The central role of the Kingdom of God (what I have renamed as the *Companionship of Empowerment*) has become a theological catalyst today for scholars and rank-and-file Christians alike. Understood to be the core truth of our faith, more Christians are realizing how extensively we have compromised this central faith conviction to accommodate ecclesiastical power collusions down through the centuries. And many of the dualistic splits between insiders and outsiders are seen to be the consequence of this theological neglect. Reappropriating the primacy of the Kingdom is precisely what inspires, motivates, and unites many contemporary Christians seeking the inclusivity explored in this book.

One senses that the newly emerging passion for greater inclusivity will win out in the end. Our world is becoming increasingly interconnected, and precisely for that reason, people feel more intensely the barriers that still divide and alienate. With such secular impetus for a more empowering inclusivity, it is anomalous that churches and religions should still be clinging on to inherited exclusions. The credibility of the Christian Gospel is at stake, and the continued failure of Christian churches to assume the challenge just alienates people further from a wonderful treasure waiting to be rediscovered.

Notes

Chapter 1

[1] For contemporary usage of the concept, particularly by Israel and by the United States, see the valuable overview by Gitlin and Leibovitz (2010).

Chapter 2

[1] British Scripture scholar, John Nolland (2004) argues that Jesus is merely reiterating a teaching that had a number of historical precedents. The Babylonian text the *Counsels of Wisdom* contains a similar call as does the Egyptian *Instruction of Amenemope*. In Greek and Roman philosophy, the idea of loving one's enemies is strongly supported. The Greek stoics expressed similar dicta of universal love. The Eastern faiths of Buddhism and Taoism also share this outlook.

[2] John Piper (1979, 17) claims that the New Testament basis for nonviolence should be sought in the early writings of St. Paul (e.g., 1 Thess. 5:15 and Rom. 12:14, 17–20). These texts explicitly command that we should not pay back evil with evil, as does 1 Peter 3:9. Piper, having traced the notion of enemy-love in the Old Testament and in Hellenistic sources (1979, 19–48), goes on to suggest that it differs from Jesus' command in that the former was given with specific qualifications or exceptions. In contrast, the command of enemy-love in early Christianity

establishes without equivocation or qualification the requirement not to repay evil with evil, but to do good, to bless the adversary. (Piper 1979, 49–65).

[3] The new translation of the Catholic Missal, introduced in English and Spanish speaking realms in December 2012, is inundated with imperial lingo, with God and Jesus frequently addressed in majestic, regal terms, and church authorities exalted to fresh patriarchal status.

Chapter 3

[1] In general, there were three areas where ritual purity was to be observed: (1) purifying the body and hands; (2) purifying vessels used for food preparation and serving; and (3) eating only pure animals. Some ways in which impurity could be contracted were through a corpse, a leper, a victim of a deadly illness, the carcass of an animal, menstruation and childbirth, sexual relations, eating unclean animals, and using ritually impure vessels. Several Scripture scholars follow the line adopted by Marcus Borg, claiming that Jesus departed significantly from ritual practices and strongly denounced the use of purity codes to exclude people in a range of different ways. John P. Meier (2009, 413–15) argues that Jesus never pronounces on the matter as if it were of no consequence for him—does this mean that Jesus undermined the ritual preoccupation precisely by ignoring its impact? Scholars such as E. P. Sanders (1985), Hyam Maccoby (1999), Jonathan Klawans (2005), and Amy-Jill Levine (2007, 2014) tend to downplay the significance of ritual purity in the time of Jesus, claiming that it was primarily a requirement for priests in relation to their temple duties. Others argue that it was a particular preoccupation of the group known as the Pharisees and should not be extended to Jewish people in general. Despite such reservations, the majority of scholars seem to consider ritual purity a substantial cultural and religious issue that was the basis of several challenges from Jesus seeking to promote and establish a culture of greater inclusivity.

[2] In May 2014, the contemporary world witnessed a vivid example of the honor/same dichotomy when a Pakistani father, accompanied by other close family relatives, bludgeoned to death his daughter because she had married a man of her own choice. What made this event particularly barbaric was the fact that it happened in public outside a top court building in Lahore, with allegedly police watching on, but taking

no protective action. Although such brutal ideological force may not have been evidenced in the time of Jesus, the event highlights the cultural and religious significance of the honor/shame dynamic.

Chapter 4

[1] On May 26, 2014, Pope Francis visited Israel and in a conversation with the Israeli Prime Minister, Benjamin Netanyahu, exchanged opinions about the original language spoken by the historical Jesus. Israeli linguistics professor Ghil'ad Zuckermann told Reuters that both Netanyahu and Pope Francis had a point. "Jesus was a native Aramaic speaker," he said about the largely defunct Semitic language closely related to Hebrew. "But he would have also known Hebrew because there were extant religious writings in Hebrew." Ghil'ad Zuckermann is professor of Linguistics and Endangered Languages for the Australian Research Council (ARC), and works at the University of Adelaide, Australia (http://www.zuckermann.org/).

Chapter 5

[1] As noted by Cresswell (2013, 137), Matthew and Luke also omit the reference to Jesus' anger in the story of the man with the withered hand (Matt. 12:10–14; Luke 6:6–11).

Chapter 6

[1] In the Catholic Eucharist, we have a double Epiclesis. First, the Holy Spirit is invoked to come down and change the elements of bread and wine into the body and blood of Christ. The second invocation is on the gathered body of participants that they may be more united as a worshipping community. There are several dualistic elements in these formulations that need to be rectified through updating the language we use. Invoking the Holy Spirit to come "down" is reminiscent of the old three-tier cosmology, which has long become redundant. Dualistic splitting is also at play in the invitation to the Holy Spirit to "change" the elements, from something inferior (secular/materialistic) to something holy, worthy of divine embodiment. All the food of creation is already sacred and fused with the energy of God's Holy Spirit. It is actually blasphemous to invoke the Holy Spirit to make holy that which is already sacred. Rather, the invocation should be primarily for the gathering people so that under the inspiration of the Holy Spirit,

they can comprehend more readily the sacredness that is already there in all God's gifts, particularly in God's daily gift of food.

Chapter 8

[1] Worthy of note however is Wendy Cotter's astute observation that those who confront Jesus with a plea for healing do so with courage and conviction far beyond what was culturally accepted at the time, and Jesus never disapproves (Cotter 2010, 7–9, 66, 74, 134, 146ff., 254). Cotter (2010, 256) concludes: "The petitioners remain spunky, pushy and outrageous. Jesus meets them on their own ground and moves to their side, recognizing their need, their confidence and the rightness of radical resolution when salvation from disease, demons, death or danger is within reach."

[2] The following are the groups listed on map that Neyrey refers to:

1. Dead Israelites: concern over Jesus' dead body (John 19:31);
2. Morally unclean Israelites: tax collectors and sinners (Luke 15:1–2; Matt. 9:10–13);
3. Bodily unclean Israelites: lepers (Mark 1:400–45; Luke 17:11–14), poor, lame, maimed, blind (Luke 14:13; see Lev. 21:18–21), menstruants (Mark 5:24–34);
4. Unobservant Israelites: Peter and John (Acts 4:13), Jesus (John 7:15, 49);
5. Observant Israelites: the rich young man (Mark 23:50–51), Joseph of Arimathea (Luke 2:25–38);
6. Pharisees (Mark 7:3–5; Luke 18:11–12);
7. Scribes and priests (Luke 10:31–32);
8. Chief priests (John 18:28; Heb. 7:18–28).

Chapter 9

[1] Worthy of note as well is that it seems to have been fear of the crowd that provoked Herod to execute John the Baptist. In his Jewish Antiquities (18.116–19) Josephus writes, "When others too joined the crowds about him, because they were aroused to the highest degree by his sermons, Herod became alarmed. Eloquence that had so great an effect on mankind might lead to some form of sedition, for it looked as if they would be guided by John in everything that they did."

Chapter 10

¹ It may be helpful here to remind the reader of the Levitical laws governing purity issues at the time of Jesus—acknowledging the fact that some Jewish scholars challenge how they were interpreted and applied in early Christian times. According to the Bible, a woman is impure for seven days from the beginning of her menstrual flow (Lev. 12:2, 15:19). Anyone who touches a menstruating woman becomes unclean until evening (Lev. 15:19). Whoever touches her bed or anything she sits on during the week is unclean until evening and must wash his clothes and bathe with water (Lev. 15:20–23).

After her menstrual cycle, a woman was required to bathe herself from head to toe in a special pool of clean water, called a *mikveh*. Each small community would have its *mikveh*, and towns and cities had large numbers of them, some public, some private. The *mikveh* pool had to be designed and built a special way, so that it had (1) enough headroom under water to allow complete immersion; (2) a supplementary tank for gathering clean rain water; and (3) a small pool at the entrance for washing hair, hands and feet before entering the main pool. The purpose of the monthly bathing in the *mikveh* was for physical and spiritual cleanliness. The washing of the body was a tangible way for a woman to renew herself, refreshing mental, emotional, and physical energies. It was a ritual that periodically gave a woman the feeling of a fresh start.

Chapter 12

¹ It is estimated that Jews in preexilic times numbered around 150,000, which grew to an estimated 8 million by the first Christian century. However, 2 to 7 million lived in the Diaspora, mainly in Rome and Alexandria.

² Hence the opening words of a recent monograph (Holmen 2011, ix) on the centrality of Judaism for our understanding of the mission of Jesus: "For some considerable time, the phrase, 'Jesus within Judaism' has both epitomized and determined the basic starting and vantage point of all historical Jesus research. Jesus should be studied and understood within Judaism, not in contrast with it."

³ Juho Sankamo (2012, 123) suggests that the following Gospel texts should be read inclusively and not exclusively: Mark 3:7–8; Matt. 8:11–12/Luke 13:28–29; Mark 13:26–27; Luke 14:15–24/Matt. 22:1–10).

Works Cited

Armstrong, Karen. 2011. *Twelve Steps to a Compassionate Life*. New York: Anchor.

Assmann, Jon. 2010. *The Price of Monotheism*. Stanford, CA: Stanford University Press.

Balslev, Anindita, and Dirk Evers. 2010. *Compassion in the World's Religions: Envisioning Human Solidarity*. Berlin: Lit Verlag.

Barker, Graeme. 2009. *The Agricultural Revolution in Prehistory*. Oxford: Oxford University Press.

Bibliowicz, Abel M. 2013. *Jews and Gentiles in the Early Christian Movement*. London: Palgrave Macmillan.

Borg, Marcus. 1994a. *Jesus in Contemporary Scholarship*. Valley Forge, PA: Trinity Press International.

———. 1994b. *Meeting Jesus Again for the First Time*. San Francisco: HarperSanFrancisco.

Borg, Marcus, and John D. Crossan. 2006. *The Last Week*. New York: HarperCollins.

———. 2009. *The First Paul*. New York: HarperCollins.

Bourgeault, Cynthia. 2008, *The Wisdom Jesus*. Boston: Shambala.

Boyarin, Daniel. 1994. *A Radical Jew*. Berkeley: University of California Press.

Breuggemann, Walter. 2005. *The Book That Breathes New Life*. Minneapolis: Fortress Press.

Brock, Rita N. 1992. *Journeys by Heart: A Christology of Erotic Power*. New York: Crossroad.

Butler, Judith. 2008. *Gender Trouble: Feminism and the Subversion of Identity*. New York and London: Routledge.

Cahill, Lisa S. 1994. *Love Your Enemies: Discipleship, Pacifism and Just War Theory*. Minneappolis: Fortress Press.

Carter, Warren. 1996. "Getting Martha Out of the Kitchen: Luke 10:38–42." *Catholic Biblical Quarterly* 58:264–80.

Casey, Maurice. 2010. *Jesus of Nazareth*. New York: Continuum.

Cook, Michael J. 2008. *Modern Jews Engage the New Testament*. Woodstock, VT: Jewish Lights Publishing.

Copeland, M. Shawn. 2010. *Enfleshing Freedom: Body, Race and Being*. Minneapolis: Fortress Press.

Corley, Kathleen. 2002. *Women and the Historical Jesus*. Santa Rosa, CA: Polebridge Press.

Cotter, Wendy. 2010. *The Christ of the Miracle Stories*. Grand Rapids: Baker Academic.

Craffert, Pieter. 2008. *The Life of a Galilean Shaman*. Eugene, OR: Cascade Books.

Cresswell, Peter. 2013. *The Invention of Jesus*. London: Watkins Publishing.

Crossan, John Dominic. 1991. *The Historical Jesus*. San Francisco: HarperSanFrancisco.

———. 1994. *In Parables*. Santa Rosa, CA: Polebridge Press.

———. 2010. *The Greatest Prayer*. New York: Harper Collins.

———. 2012. *The Power of Parable*. New York: HarperCollins.

Crossan, John Dominic, and Jonathan L. Reed. 2004. *Excavating Paul*. San Francisco: HarperSanFrancisco.

Dodd, C. H. 1978. *The Parables of the Kingdom*. London: Fontana/Fount.

Drake-Brockman, Tom. 2012. *Christian Humanism: The Compassionate Theology of a Jew Called Jesus*. Sydney: Denis Jones and Associates.

Dunn, James G. D. 1990. *Unity and Diversity in the New Testament*, London: SCM Press.

Edser, Stuart. 2012. *Being Gay, Being Christian*. Wollumbi, NSW: Exisle Publishing.

Edwards, Denis. 2004. *Breath of the Spirit*. Maryknoll, NY: Orbis Books.

Ehrman, Bart. 2011. *The New Testament: A Historical Introduction to the Early Christian Writings*. New York: Oxford University Press.

Eisler, Riane. 1989. *The Chalice and the Blade*. New York: Harper and Row.

Eisler, Philip Francis. 1987. "Table Fellowship." In *Community and Gospel in Luke-Acts*, 71–109. Cambridge: Cambridge University Press.

Farley, Wendy. 2011. *Gathering Those Driven Away: A Theology of Incarnation*. Louisville, KY: WJK Press.

Ferder, Fran, and John Heagle. 2002. *Tender Fires: The Spiritual Promise of Sexuality*. New York: Crossroad.

Forest, Jim. 2014. *Loving Our Enemies: Reflections on the Hardest Commandment*. Maryknoll, NY: Orbis Books.

Funk, Robert. 1996. *Honest to Jesus*. San Francisco: HarperSanFrancisco.

Gagnon, Robert. 2001. *The Bible and Homosexual Practice*, Nashville: Abingdon Press.

Garber, Zev. 2011. *The Jewish Jesus*. West Lafayete, IN: Purdue University Press.

Gitlin, Todd, and Liel Leibovitz. 2013. *The Chosen Peoples: America, Israel, and the Ordeals of Divine Election*. New York: Simon and Schuster.

Gonzalez, Antonio. 2012. *God's Reign and the End of Empires*. Miami, FL: Convivium Press.

Goosen, Gideon. 2011. *Hyphenated Christians*. New York: Peter Lang.

Halperin, David. 1989. *One Hundred Years of Homosexuality: And Other Essays on Greek Love (New Ancient World)*. New York and London: Routledge.

Herzog, William. 1994. *Parables as Subversive Speech*. Louisville, KY: Westminster/John Knox Press.

Holmen, Tom, ed. 2011. *Jesus in Continuum*. Tubingen, Germany: Mohr Siebeck.

hooks, bell. 2004. "Choosing the Margin as a Space of Radical Openness." In *The Feminist Standpoint Theory Reader: Intellectual and Political Controversies*, ed. S. Harding, 153–59. New York: Routledge.

Horsley, Richard. 2003. *Jesus and Empire*. Minneapolis: Fortress Press.

Humphreys, Colin J. 2011. *The Mystery of the Last Supper*. Cambridge (UK): Cambridge University Press.

Hylen, Susan E. 2014. "The Domestication of Saint Thecla," *Journal of Feminist Studies in Religion*. 30:2, 5-21.

Jennings, Theodore. 2003. *The Man Jesus Loved*. Cleveland: Pilgrim Press.

Jeremias, Joachim. 1958. *Jesus' Promise to the Nations*. London: SCM Press.

Johnson, Kurt, and David Robert Ord. 2012. *The Coming Interspiritual Age*. Vancouver: Namaste Publishing.

Karris, Robert J. 1985 "The Theme of Food." In *Luke: Artist and Theologian*, 47–78. New York: Paulist Press.

Klawans, Jonathan. 2005. *Purity, Sacrifice and the Temple*. New York: Oxford University Press.

Kraybill, Donald B. 1990. *The Upside Down Kingdom*. Scottdale, PA: Herald Press.

Lawrence, Louise J. 2013. *Sense and Stigma in the Gospels*. Oxford: Oxford University Press.

Levine, Amy-Jill. 2007. *The Misunderstood Jew*. New York: HarperOne.

———. 2014. *Short Stories by Jesus: The Enigmatic Parables of a Controversial Rabbi*. New York: HarperOne.

Maccoby, Hyam. 1999. *Ritual and Morality: The Ritual Purity System and Its Place in Judaism*. Cambridge: Cambridge University Press.

Malina, Bruce J. 2001. *The New Testament World: Insights from Cultural Anthropology*. Louisville, KY: Westminster/John Knox Press.

Marion, Jim. 2000. *Putting on the Mind of Christ*. Charlottesville, VA: Hampton Roads Publishing.

Meier, John. P. 2009. *A Marginal Jew: Rethinking the Historical Jesus*, vol.2/vol.4. New Haven, CT: Yale University Press.

Moss, Candida. 2013. *The Myth of Persecution*. New York: HarperCollins.

Moxnes, Halvor. 1987. "Meals and the New Community in Luke." *Svensk Exegetisk Årsbok* 51:158–67.

Neyrey, Jerome H. 1991 "Ceremonies in Luke-Acts: The Case of Meals and Table Fellowship." In *The Social World of*

Luke-Acts. Models for Interpretation, 361–87. Peabody, MA: Hendrikson Publishers.

———. 1996. "Meals, Food and Table Fellowship in the New Testament." In *The Social Sciences and the New Testament*, ed. Richard L. Rohrbaugh, 159–82. Peabody, MA: Hendrickson Publishers.

———. 1998. *Honor and Shame in the Gospel of Matthew*. Louisville, KY: Westminster Press.

Nolland, John. 2004. "The Mandate: Love Our Enemies." *Anvil* 21:23–33.

Novak, David. 1995. *The Election of Israel*. Cambridge: Cambridge University Press.

O'Connell, Maureen. 2009. *Compassion*. New York: Orbis Books.

Olyan, Saul. 2008. Disability in the Hebrew Bible. New York: Cambridge University Press.

O'Murchu, Diarmuid. 2002. *Evolutionary Faith*. Maryknoll, NY: Orbis Books.

———. 2011. *Christianity's Dangerous Memory*. New York: Crossroad.

———. 2012. *In the Beginning Was the Spirit: Science, Religion, and Indigenous Spirituality*. Maryknoll, NY: Orbis Books.

———. 2014. *On Being a Postcolonial Christian*. North Charleston, SC: CreateSpace.

Page, Nick. 2011. *The Wrong Messiah*. London: Hodder & Stoughton.

Park, Eung Chun. 2003. *Either Jew or Gentile: Paul's Unfolding Theology of Inclusivity*. Louisville, KY: Westminster/John Knox Press.

Pederson, Rena. 2006. *The Lost Apostle: Searching for the Truth about Junia*. San Francisco: Wiley.

Piper, John. 1979. *Love Your Enemies*. Cambridge: Cambridge University Press.

Plumwood, Val. 2002. *Environmental Culture: The Ecological Crisis of Reason*. New York: Routledge.

Ricoeur, Paul. 1976. *Interpretation Theory: Discourse and the Surplus of Meaning*. Fort Worth: Texas Christian University Press.

Runesson, Anna. 2011. *Exegesis in the Making: Postcolonialism and New Testament Studies*. Leiden,The Netherlands: Brill.

Sanders, E. P. 1985. *Jesus and Judaism*. Philadelphia: Fortress Press.

Sankamo, Juho. 2012. *Jesus and the Gentiles*. Abo, Finland: Abo Akademi University Press.

Schaberg, Jane. 1992. "Luke." In *The Women's Bible Commentary*, ed. Carol A. Newsom and Sharon H. Ringe, 257–92. Louisville, KY: Westminster/John Knox Press.

Schneiders, Sandra. 1999. *The Revelatory Text*, Collegeville, MN: Liturgical Press.

Schussler Fiorenza, Elizabeth. 1983. *In Memory of Her*. New York: Crossroad.

———. 2001. *Wisdom Ways: Introducing Feminist Biblical Interpretation*. Maryknoll, NY: Orbis Books.

Sedgwick, Eve Kosofsky. 2008. *Epistemology of the Closet*. Oakland: University of California Press.

Shinan, Avigdor, and Yair Zakovitch. 2012. *From Gods to God*. Philadelphia: Jewish Publication Society.

Smith, Dennis E. 2003. *From Symposium to Eucharist*. Minneapolis: Fortress Press.

Spina, Frank Anthony. 2006. *The Faith of the Outsider: Exclusion and Inclusion in the Biblical Story*. Grand Rapids: Eerdmans.

Stamm, Mark W. 2006. *Let Every Soul Be Jesus' Guest, A Theology of the Open Table* Nashville: Abingdon.

Stormer Hanson, Mary. 2013. *The New Perspective on Mary and Martha*. Eugene, OR: Wipf & Stock.

Tausig, Hal. 2009. *In the Beginning Was the Meal*. Minneapolis: Fortress Press.

Thistlethwaite, Susan B. 2013. *Occupy the Bible*. Eugene, OR: Wipf & Stock.

Vondey, Wolfgang. 2010. *Beyond Pentecostalism*. Grand Rapids: Eerdmans.

Wink, Walter. 1992. *Engaging the Powers*. Minneapolis: Fortress.

———. 2002. *The Human Being: Jesus and the Enigma of the Son of Man*. Minneapolis: Augsburg Fortress.

Yong, Amos. 2010. *In the Days of Caesar: Pentecostalism and Political Theology*. Grand Rapids: Eerdmans.

Znamenski, Andrei. 2007. *The Beauty of the Primitive: Shamanism and the Western Imagination*. New York: Oxford University Press.

Index